THE SIX-MINUTE MEMOIR

For Alane—
With thanks &
good wishes,
Mary Helen

A BUR OAK BOOK
Holly Carver, series editor

THE SIX-MINUTE MEMOIR

MARY HELEN STEFANIAK

FIFTY-FIVE SHORT ESSAYS ON LIFE

UNIVERSITY OF IOWA PRESS | IOWA CITY

University of Iowa Press, Iowa City 52242

Copyright © 2022 by Mary Helen Stefaniak

uipress.uiowa.edu

ISBN 978-1-60938-851-5 (pbk)

ISBN 978-1-60938-852-2 (ebk)

Printed in the United States of America

Cover design by Kimberly Glyder

Text design and typesetting by April Leidig

Printed on acid-free paper

Cataloging-in-Publication data is on file with the Library of Congress.

Madeline DeFrees, excerpts from "In the locker room" and "In the middle of Priest Lake." From *Blue Dusk: New and Selected Poems, 1951–2001* by Madeline DeFrees. Copyright © 1991 by Madeline DeFrees. Reprinted with the permission of The Permissions Company, LLC, on behalf of Copper Canyon Press, coppercanyonpress.org.

Czeslaw Milosz, "Six Lectures in Verse: Lecture IV." From *New and Collected Poems: 1931–2001* by Czeslaw Milosz. Copyright ©1988, 1991, 1995, 2001 by Czeslaw Milosz Royalties, Inc. Used by permission of HarperCollins Publishers.

For everyone who appears in these pages,
whether by name, anonymously, or in disguise

CONTENTS

MY BRAIN EVENT

A NOTE TO READERS ABOUT
WHAT YOU'LL FIND IN THIS BOOK

In 1998, while I was working hard every day on what I hoped would become my first novel, the editor of the *Iowa Source* invited me to write a monthly column for her magazine, which is distributed free in Iowa and to subscribers in other parts of the world. Claudia had previously published an essay I wrote about serving as a chaperone for my daughter's high school show choir on a road trip to New Orleans, which included an eighteen-hour bus ride each way and three days (or was it three weeks?) at a hotel in the French Quarter.

Writing regularly for "Iowa's Enlightening Magazine" would give me a substantial local audience—more than twenty thousand readers—including the kind of readers who recognize the name on your credit card or (in the old days) on your check at the grocery store and say things like, "Aren't you the writer?" and "I loved the one about scuba diving!" The *Iowa Source* has been published without a break since it was founded in 1984 in Fairfield, Iowa, a unique community of about ten thousand in the southeastern corner of the state. When I asked editor and publisher Claudia Mueller how she has managed to keep the magazine alive and well for more than thirty-seven years now, she said, "We've had to constantly adapt to changes, rethinking and refining our content when necessary. The monthly format is perfect for that, and it's been fun to reinvent the *Source* over the years."

Despite the potential readership, not to mention monthly opportunities for reinvention, my first thought about writing a column was *Are you kidding? I'm trying to write a novel here.* I already had a full-time teaching job getting in the way. Trying to save a few hours each day to inch the novel forward seemed impossible enough without taking a break every month to write something else.

Something short.

Something with an end in sight.

By the time my novel came out in 2004, it was obvious to me that my ability to finish the darn thing depended in large part—thank you, Claudia!—on those monthly breaks to write something short, something with an end in sight. Claudia said I could write about anything I wanted. Like a lot of people—Henry James and Anaïs Nin, to name just two—I had notebooks full of observations and descriptions and overheard conversations and deep thoughts and surprising things my children and (eventually, though not yet in 1998 or even 2004) my grandchildren had said. I thought of these notebooks as inventory for my fiction, and I have, in fact, used much of the material that way. The notebooks were also a place to record and save experiences that I didn't have a use for but didn't want to lose, experiences that seemed significant enough to write down. As a monthly columnist, I had a place (and a deadline) to put them down on the page in a thousand words or so, which happens to be about the number of words you can read aloud at a conversational pace in six minutes.

I don't remember how Dennis Reese at Iowa Public Radio discovered my column. He might have picked up a copy of the *Iowa Source* with his coffee one morning, and after reading one of my pieces—maybe "Airborne in the Dairy Section" or "Ducklings on Dodge" or "The Right Clothes"—he might have thought, *Hey! This would make a great radio commentary.* Or I might have sent him a couple of samples and a pleading query letter. One way or the other, I ended up reading many of these pieces as six-minute spots on Iowa Public Radio.

In *I Could Tell You Stories*, Patricia Hampl wrote, "Stalking the relationship, seeking the congruence between stored image and hidden emotion—that's the real job of memoir." I don't know how much stalking I have done here. Almost every "stored image" I came up with as I wrote these pages seemed to explain—to me, if to no one else—the extent to which I was and continue to be *Alive and Well (In the Middle of the Middle West)*, which is what we called the column. The "hidden emotion" to be found in most of these pages was best described by a regular reader of my column—a retired professor of law, no less—who remarked, "How much fun she has in her life! Then she writes it all down, and I get to enjoy it, too." (See "*Who Cares, Anyway?* Diary of a School Age Romantic.")

I don't know if fun counts as a hidden emotion, the kind you might stalk in memoir, but I do know how surprised—and pleased—I was by that reader's comment. Bad and sad things happened to me, and to others I care about, during the years when I wrote my column, but the things that came to mind whenever I started assembling one of these little essays were the kinds of things we find ourselves wanting to share with someone else because we find them interesting, or even remarkable, worth remembering, and, more often than not, funny.

I like to think that I'm following in the footsteps of a writer I first encountered a few years ago while teaching World Lit I: Gilgamesh to Shakespeare. Sei Shōnagon, author of *The Pillow Book*, filled her pages with six- and five- and three- and two- and even one-minute memoirs: scenes and images, anecdotes, descriptions, lists, flashes of poetry, and her thoughts about what it was like to be a lady at court in tenth-century Japan. My six-minute memoirs offer glimpses of what it was like to be a woman with a family and friends and a job (more than one job, actually) and a series of cats and a history, living in one old house after another at the turn of the twenty-first century in the middle of the Middle West.

Some years ago, I taught a class for the Senior Center in Iowa City. It was a writing class. The idea was to capture a place, a person, a moment, or even an object, a practice, a process plucked from your personal past and save it from oblivion by putting it vividly on the page. If you were going to write about baking biscuits with your grandmother (and I remember that a woman in the class did just that), then you wanted to make your readers smell and maybe taste those biscuits, you wanted to show your grandmother's hand pressing the rim of a glass into the flattened and floury dough. Maybe you could even capture her voice. As she handed you the glass to cut the next biscuit, did she say, "Careful, careful now!" or "Cut closer to the other circles—don't waste so much," or "You try it now—it's easy!"? Or did she tell you other things, what life was like when she was a girl and later a mother, things she hoped for, things she loved (or hated) to do, things that made her happy, things that broke her heart?

The idea, in other words, was to write your own two- or four- or six-minute memoir and then read it to the class the following week.

Some of the writers in the class wanted specific assignments: describe the first kitchen you can remember. Tell us about a time when you had to sit very still. Introduce us to a pet who gave you love and trouble. Take us on a trip you took. Remember your most memorable teacher.

Others came already equipped with lists of memories they wanted to share with their children or grandchildren or great-grandchildren. Either way, the secret to success—to winning our rapt attention, our nods of recognition, our exclamations of surprise or sympathy, even eruptions of laughter—seemed to be in finding the details, all those "stored images," and following the path they put down for you as you put them on the page.

That's what I've tried to do in each of the essays in this book. I hope you enjoy them. And if you feel inspired to *write* a six-minute memoir, I invite you to peruse the prompts that follow the last essay in the book. Any one of them might open the door to your own stash of stored images and set you on your path down the page.

A SAMPLER

AQUILA NON CAPIT MUSCAS

Puttin' on the Drake

In January, my husband, John, had two brilliant ideas.
The first one was to spend a night at The Drake Hotel, which
is where the Emperor of Japan, the King of Sweden, and the
Queen of England stay when they are in Chicago. Of course, kings
and queens have financial resources—national treasuries and the
like—that make the place almost affordable. For my husband and
me, even one night was an outrageous extravagance.

"Come on," John said. "It's your birthday."

This was, coincidentally, true. I was scheduled to read at the
Newberry Library in Chicago on the night before my birthday,
but I also had a class to teach in Cedar Rapids at noon the next
day. I voted for driving to Chicago and coming back the same
night.

"But you're reading at the *Newberry*," John said.

Twenty years ago, on his first visit to the Newberry, a library
that houses a research collection of rare books and manuscripts,
my husband had been politely asked to leave. (Not only was he
not a member, but he had wandered in looking for a current issue
of *Car and Driver.*) For John, my reading there was his chance to
return in triumph.

"What better occasion will we ever have to stay at The Drake?"
he asked me.

Any occasion that involved the receipt of large sums of
money—selling film rights, for example, or winning the lottery—
would have been better. I agreed, however, that a reservation
might be wise *just in case* the weather went bad. We had until late
afternoon to cancel without charge.

The snow started as we left Iowa City Wednesday morning and stayed with us all the long, slow way to Chicago. By the time we reached downtown, I would have paid even more than we ended up paying, just to get out of the car NOW, not to mention having a guy in a greatcoat take our keys at the curb, give us a receipt for "three pieces of luggage," and hand us over to the doorman at The Drake.

In the lobby, the desk clerk did not so much as let her eyes linger on my husband's untied tennis shoes or the indelible ink stain on the left front pocket of his canvas coat. (In places like The Drake, they train the help not to stare.) She gave us a form to sign and exchanged our luggage receipt for two cardkeys to room 840, neatly enclosed in a little white folder with "A Short History of Chicago's Most Famous Hotel" and an explanation of the coat-of-arms motto, "Aquila Non Capit Muscas," which means, "An eagle does not catch flies." A bell attendant would meet us upstairs, she said.

We crossed the lobby, pretending not to be impressed by a fresh flower arrangement the size of a Christmas tree. Waiting for the elevator, I'm afraid my eyes did linger on my husband's untied tennis shoes. "You know," I said as the doors glided open, "when Sting stays at The Drake, he probably dresses just like that."

"Like what?" replied my husband.

In the elevator was a little upholstered bench. We sat on it.

When we reached the eighth floor and looked down the hall to our right, we saw tall white double doors guarded by a young man in uniform, his white-gloved hands folded in front of him. On a rolling rack beside the young man were our three pieces of luggage: my gym bag, John's gym bag (which doesn't zip shut), and three shirts on a hanger.

Lucky for our charge card balance, it wasn't the bridal suite—just your ordinary deluxe hotel room equipped with a desk full of Drake stationery (including picture postcards of the flower arrangement in the lobby), a wet bar tastefully disguised as a closet, and, in the bathroom, a white terrycloth robe with a Drake dragon embroidered on the pocket. After opening the door for us, the bell attendant hung John's shirts in the real closet and swept back the drapes to reveal an eighth-floor view of slate-gray lake and snow-covered beach cradled in the sweeping curve of Lake Shore Drive. Figuring that Wednesdays in January were a little slow at The Drake, we tipped the young man generously.

The reading that night was great: a full house, free wine and cheese, and plenty of opportunity for John to strut around the Newberry lobby as if he owned the joint. (This time no one asked him, "Are you a member, sir?") Back at The Drake, I slipped into the white terrycloth robe, and we enjoyed the lake view, resisting the temptation to help ourselves to a tiny bottled beverage or snack from the closet bar. (Would the Emperor of Japan plunk down that much for a Snickers, we wondered?) We had a 4:30 wake-up call to get us out of the Loop before rush hour, and we would have made it, if not for one unfortunate detail. When we gave the first guy in the greatcoat our car keys, everything was A-OK with our twenty-five-year-old Volvo. In the morning, when another guy (probably in the same greatcoat) brought it back, the red light was on.

This was a familiar problem, indicative of a blown fuse and/or a short in the circuit that meant the battery was not recharging and we would soon be rolling to a dead-battery stop. Sadly, we had already made the turn onto Michigan Avenue before we noticed the red light. John pulled over promptly into the bus lane. All we needed to fix the car—for now anyway—was a fuse and a flashlight. We had a box of fuses stowed between the seats. The flashlight was on top of the refrigerator at home.

John needed only a minute with his head on the driver's seat and his legs sticking out into the bus lane to confirm his suspicion that he couldn't change one in a long line of fuses cloaked in utter darkness under the dashboard. Minutes ticked by. Buses had begun to appear, growling up behind our little car and swinging around it, one after the other, inches from my husband's untied tennis shoes, when he was struck—not by a bus, but by his second brilliant idea of the month.

Remember how the Apollo astronauts bounced the rays of the sun off the palms of their shiny gloves onto the dark side of the lunar module, using the sun for a flashlight on the moon? It turns out you can do the same thing with the mirror in my CoverGirl compact and a nearby streetlight. John got me to class in Cedar Rapids on Thursday with minutes to spare. Hey. An eagle does not catch flies.

POSITIVELY 4TH STREET

Where Mothers Rule

MAY 1998

Where I grew up—in a working-class neighborhood in Milwaukee, some years ago—mothers were not much like the mothers you see today, assuming you look fast enough to catch us before we drop the kids off and drive away to work, drinking our coffee or making last-minute phone calls as we go.

The mothers on 4th Street were like God: all-knowing, all-present, all-powerful, and most of the time unseen. Their most apparent role in the flow of neighborhood life was calling kids in. They called us in to eat supper, to go somewhere (like Sears on Mitchell Street or my grandmother's house), to practice (usually the accordion), to do our homework, or to take a bath and go to bed. No matter where we were—down by the creek, at the corner store, in the field behind John Greenleaf Whittier School, or in Judene Szweda's attic, which could be reached only by a ladder that led to a trapdoor in the ceiling of the Szwedas' bathroom—our mothers always knew where to find us. If we strayed beyond the range of their call, then somebody else would hear it and pass it along: "Hey! Mary Helen! Your mom's calling you."

After I grew up and went to college, I learned that the mothers on 4th Street (and across the alley on 3rd) were oppressed by society and by their working-class husbands, who demanded that women stay home, take care of the children, and have supper ready and waiting when the men got home from work. Growing up, I confess, I saw the situation differently. The way I saw it, men had to go to work, the same way kids had to go to school. Since

I did not aspire to a job as a welder at Ladish Manufacturing or a spot on the assembly line at Allen-Bradley (to be honest, I did not aspire to doing anything that somebody else told me to do for eight hours a day), it seemed to me that mothers were the lucky ones. They got to stay home.

At home, the mothers were in charge. The fathers were like visitors — only more exhausted and less polite. Fathers were significant chiefly as chauffeurs (since most mothers couldn't drive) on their days off. Then they became repairmen, plumbers, carpenters, painters, window washers, lawn care experts (Dad's specialty), or auto mechanics, each man according to his talents and the needs of the household, which were determined, usually, by the mothers.

And what did mothers do all day in the freedom and sanctity of their homes? That, of course, I paid less attention to, being busy at school or down at the creek or at the freeway construction site, where we zoomed on makeshift skateboards down the new concrete ramps. When I picture the mothers on 4th Street, I see Mrs. Fecteau at the Singer in her dining room, sewing up a summer's worth of shorts for her four daughters while keeping an eye on her favorite soaps. (Forty years later, Mrs. Fecteau is gone, but "As the World Turns" is still on the air.) I see Mrs. Shultis on her backyard patio, hanging paper lanterns. The Shultises had the only patio on the block; they threw parties, not just baby showers.

I see Mrs. Szweda sorting clean laundry on her dining room table. (Nobody I knew used the room for dining.) I see her hanging shirts on doorknobs and drawer-pulls of the built-in buffet. Either that or peeling potatoes. She had two grown sons and a husband in the house, truck drivers all. I don't think I ever came looking for my friend Judene after school without seeing her mother in the kitchen peeling potatoes and dropping them into a freestanding cooker — like a Crockpot on wheels — about the size of a laundry tub.

Most of the mothers on 4th Street were "Mrs." but a few had

names, like my mother, who was "Mary" even to some of my friends, and Pam Dragan's mother, Connie. Recently I noticed this: the mothers with names were the ones who had jobs. Both my mother and Connie Dragan were waitresses, Mom part-time at the Tasty Town lunch counter in Gimbels and Connie at The Bay, a restaurant run by *her* mother.

Working outside the home was a questionable pursuit in those days. One of the threats of World Communism, I recall from the 1950s, was that mothers would be forced to work outside the home and leave the raising of their children to state-run day care centers. (Can you imagine?) My mother's job was acceptable only because (a) it was part-time, (b) my sister was old enough to babysit for us, and (c) most important, there was no reason to suspect that my mother *liked* working at Tasty Town.

Connie Dragan, on the other hand, obviously enjoyed her job. I'm sure some people pursed their lips at the sight of her — running down the front steps to the car in dark stockings, red lipstick, and her crisp black and white uniform, looking far more energetic than was decent for a mother of nine (or seven or six or however many she had at the time), and leaving two or three little Dragans on the porch behind her, sad and forlorn, along with their babysitter (sometimes my sister), who looked equally forlorn.

What I remember best about my own mother getting ready for work was the way she smelled — a pleasant blend of Jergens lotion and Listerine (original flavor). Her Tasty Town uniform was a starched yellow jumper over a white blouse, with a little white apron on top of that and a white crown in her hair that made her look like Judy Garland in *The Harvey Girls*. My mother worked at Tasty Town for many years before she moved on to a fancier restaurant and better tips at the Boston Store downtown, and finally to Food Service at St. Luke's Hospital, where she worked until shortly after my father died, also at St. Luke's Hospital, in 1983. (She used to send him treats on his dinner tray.) Now she volunteers there. Every year, around Christmas time, she puts some thought into what she'll wear to the Volunteer Recognition Dinner. Occasionally, she buys a new outfit—something mothers seldom did during the years we lived on 4th Street. Listerine and lotion she still keeps on hand.

Now that I think about it, Mrs. Szweda also had a job, on top of all the laundry and potatoes. She played the clarinet in a four-piece band that used to practice in her living room. They did weddings and anniversaries, Holy Name Society smokers, things like that.

Mrs. Szweda's name, I remember, was Irene.

GREAT AUNTS

From the Family Tree, Georgia Branch

G reat aunts like mine are hard to find. To get to my Great Aunt Mae's, for example, you take Georgia Highway 243 to the sign that says, "TURN HERE for Mount Pleasant Baptist Church." Turn there, but when you get to Mount Pleasant Baptist Church, go right on past it and around the bend until you get to a second little white church. The African Methodist Episcopal. Just beyond it, on your left, is a dirt road. Follow that dirt road until it ends in a cloud of red dust in Aunt Mae's front yard. Important: don't get out of your car until Aunt Mae comes out with a stick to calm the dogs down.

I'd never met Aunt Mae before the road trip we took last August. Three generations of us—my mother, my sister and I, my teen-aged daughter Lauren, and my son, Jeff—journeyed to Milledgeville, Georgia, where Mom and her sisters went to high school with famous author Flannery O'Connor. We stayed at the Holiday Inn, right across the road from the farm where O'Connor wrote stories and raised peacocks. From there, we fanned out to surrounding towns—Gordon, Haddock, Gray—to visit relatives I hadn't seen in many years, if at all. Among them were three great aunts: all in their eighties and still going strong.

It took us two tries to find Aunt Mae, who, my mother told us, was renowned in her youth for her long, curly hair and a miraculous ability to take your measurements and make you a dress that looked just like the picture in the magazine. On our first attempt, we turned down the wrong dirt road. We bumped along between deep ditches under towering pines in my sister's Ford Explorer, trying not to think about the Flannery O'Connor story in which an entire family gets wiped out by escaped convicts after they turn down the wrong dirt road in Georgia.

When we finally found Aunt Mae's place, she came out to greet us, laughing and crying and waving a big stick. She ushered us inside her doublewide mobile home, where she nearly perished with delight over the birthday cake we'd brought her. Aunt Mae blew out the candles and apologized for the lack of air-conditioning, explaining that her window unit cost too much to run in really hot weather. Then she stopped in front of the couch where my son was sitting.

"Lordy, lordy!" she cried. "Is that hair I see hanging all the way down your back?" Jeff, who's twenty-three, has a ponytail he's been growing since junior high. Before he could say, "Yes, ma'am, it is," she had snatched it up and curled the end over her finger. "Look at that now," she said. "My hair used to be just like that, so long and pretty." Then she took Jeff's face in both her hands, rocked his head from side to side, and gave him a kiss on the cheek. "They all take after their Aunt Mae," she said, winking at him. "Leastwise, the good-lookin' ones do."

Compared to Aunt Mae, Great Aunt Molly was easy to find. Aunt Molly's brick ranch house and well-groomed lawn are right next door to her salvage yard on Highway 49. We found her in the kitchen, flipping corn cakes for us in a huge iron skillet, impervious to 100-degree heat. Great Aunt Molly has always been one tough cookie. Ten years ago, at the age of seventy-five, she was deer hunting on her property near Macon when she fell out of the tree she was using as a stand and broke her back. (She was lucky, she said. She could have shot her head off.) There was nobody around to help, so she crawled to her truck and drove herself into town.

At eighty-five, she still presides over the salvage business she and late Great Uncle Ebeneezer established decades ago. Great Aunt Molly has the most idyllic junkyard you could ever hope to see: nineteen acres of pecan grove traversed by sandy lanes and scattered with wrecks. Squirrels leap and scamper in the trees, leaves rustle, calico cats stalk mice and rattlesnakes from the fenders of totaled Toyotas and old Fords. And in the sagging wooden shed that serves as the office, you get to see Aunt Molly in action.

Business as usual goes like this. A guy drives up and tells the frail old woman in jeans and a flowered T-shirt that he needs a steering column for a '92 Taurus and a part for his transmission. Aunt Molly invites him to have a look around. The guy wants a price first. Aunt Molly squints at him. For the steering column, she says, "Seventy-five bucks." For the other part, well, she reckons she'd have to see it first. So the man steps outside, rummages around in a pile of parts next to the path, and pulls out something the size of a Number 2 can of peaches.

"It'll be about this big," he says, handing it to her.

Aunt Molly hefts it once or twice and says, "Ten dollars."

Great Aunts Mae and Molly married onto the family tree, but Great Aunt Aileen — who bears a strong resemblance to my mother — was born there. In a picture that my sister took this summer, Aileen and Mom are frowning at the camera like two black-eyed peas in a pod.

Back in the days when our family took a road trip to Georgia almost every year, we used to stay at Great Aunt Aileen's house in Macon — a big stucco house old enough to have a fireplace in every room and a bathroom on the back porch that you had to go outside to get to. I loved that bathroom on the back porch, the bang of the first screen door still riding the air when it was time to slam the second one. I loved the baking powder biscuits Aileen served us every morning with peach preserves and buttered grits. Great Aunt Aileen was born with a left arm that ends at the elbow, but she could roll and cut biscuits better with one hand than other people could with two. "The only thing I can't do with my one arm," Aileen liked to say, "is clap my hands." She calls my mother "May-rih," as in, "Well, May-rih, I declare!"

(Try saying it out loud—*May*-rih—and you've got yourself a middle-Georgia accent, just like that.)

Aileen's younger sister, Gladys, is the only one of my great aunts who died young—of a heart ailment in her sixties—but Great Aunt Gladys was still around when I made my last road trip to Georgia with Mom and Dad, bringing along my two little kids and a nursing baby. Neither my mother nor Aunt Gladys, being of the postwar bottle-baby school, had ever breastfed a baby, so they were a little doubtful about the whole operation, though glad to keep me company. My mother was always very discreet—it was her idea that we retire to the den, away from the menfolk—but, like the rest of my great aunts, Gladys had never been afraid to speak her mind. She blurted out what both of them were thinking when she cried, "Mary Helen, I don't see *how* you can feed that *big* ole baby with them little bitty titties!"

Great aunts like mine are hard to find.

CARDIAC DREAMS

In the Heart of the Heart of the Country

NOVEMBER 2001
With a nod to William Gass

I think I know what George Lucas was doing when he came up with the idea for Jabba the Hutt. (In case you've forgotten, Jabba the Hutt is an evil green blobby thing with terrible eating habits who captures Princess Leia and holds her hostage through most of *Return of the Jedi.*)

I'll tell you what Lucas was doing when he came up with Jabba. He was having a cardiac ultrasound. I'd bet money on it. I just had one myself, and I can tell you that the heart—projected upside down on a black-and-white computer screen with its muscle mass jiggling and rippling in time to its own beat—is a dead ringer for the pulpy, pointy-headed monster called Jabba the Hutt.

Watching my own heart beat last week, I didn't know whether to laugh or look the other way. Actually, I had to twist my head around and peer over my shoulder to see it at all. A cardiac ultrasound requires lying on your left side, facing the wall, with the ultrasound technician perched on the edge of the bed behind you, where she can use one hand to roll the probe around on your chest and the other to click away on the keyboard of the ultrasound machine, snapping pictures of your heart, looking for its good side and its bad side, if any. I kept craning my neck to see it, an astonishing little creature alive in my ribcage. It looked like an alien from another planet, a fat and slightly winded alien, breathing hard.

And the sounds it makes! My heartbeat may be a little sloshier than some due to the murmur I was having checked out at the time, but the ultrasound technician—a woman about my age—

assured me that my heart sounds were pretty typical for a woman about my age. The sound of a heart beating is less like the quick-thud, quick-thud that gets louder and louder in the 16 mm black-and-white version of *The Tell-Tale Heart* that I remember watching in high school than it is like the turntable scratching of a rap song: SshuKUNK, sshuKUNK, sshuKUNK.

Exactly the sort of sound you'd expect a dark and ripply creature trapped inside a ribcage to make.

The ultrasound technician said she used to have dreams when she first started working at the cardiac center fifteen years ago.

"Dreams about hearts?" I asked her.

"Yes," she said. "I'd wake up to that sound"—ssshuKUNK, ssshuKUNK—"and I'd see them." She shook her head and gave a little shrug.

"You'd see hearts?" I asked. "Where?"

"At the foot of the bed. In a corner. Watch out. Here comes the goop."

It was time for me to lie on my back and let her press the probe in under my ribcage for a southern exposure that gave new meaning to the phrase "from the bottom of my heart."

"That's your liver," she said, rolling the probe around.

It looked like a liver—heavy, inert, best served with onions. But there was my heart again, jollying back and forth on top of my liver like an animated beanbag or something. What a clown.

"It's a ticklish business," the technician said. "Sorry."

My heart murmur turned out to be nothing—a slurpy valve I've had since childhood that seemed a little noisier than usual, that's all—but I was glad the doctor thought it best to check it out. It's not every day you get to see your heart up close and personal like that. The only bad part of the whole experience was the television in the waiting room: the President talking at top volume about homeland security while updates on the bombing of Afghanistan moved silently across the bottom of the screen.

One thing about seeing your heart on an ultrasound is that all those "heart" expressions we use, including the ones that are likely to come up in a President's speech—heartfelt, heartland, whole-hearted—suddenly have anatomical connotations. Once you've seen that creature pulsating in your chest, you don't even want to think about wearing your heart on your sleeve.

It was a smart move George Lucas made, to take that noisy, slurpy little being and make it big and green and voracious.

Czeslaw Milosz, one of my favorite poets and a Nobel laureate to boot, has a wonderful poem that begins, "Reality, what can we do with it?" Milosz survived both world wars in eastern Europe, and in this poem, he is still

trying to save Miss Jadwiga,
A little hunchback, librarian by profession,
Who perished in the shelter of an apartment house
That was considered safe but toppled down.

"The true enemy of man"—and of woman, apparently—"is generalization," Milosz says. This is why he keeps returning to "The little skeleton of Miss Jadwiga, the spot / Where her heart was pulsating."

I wish I'd asked the ultrasound lady to tell me more about her cardiac dreams. Were they nightmarish, like Poe's story—a heart hidden under the floorboards? Or were they cute—even comical? I tried to picture such a dream. I imagined opening my eyes in the middle of the night and lying there between waking and sleeping—you know how it is—unable to move. I'd hear it first. SshuKUNK, sshuKUNK. Then I'd see it: a heart beating among the dustballs in the corner by the radiator, or rocking back and forth at the foot of the bed, or thumping away on the dresser. Not a valentine heart, and not a hard knot of muscle like the ones that come stuffed inside your Thanksgiving turkey. No. This would be a human heart, doomed but supple, oblivious to fate, sacred as the next guy's, full of treasure, brave and sweet and a little lonely, a strongly beating heart. Like hers. Like yours. Like theirs. Like mine.

THE OLD
NEIGHBORHOOD

KING OF SCROUNGE

Intimations of Immortality

Among his film and video-making friends, my son, Jeff, has had a reputation since high school for coming up with special effects on little or no budget. Only Jeff could turn a heap of broken calculators and molded Styrofoam into a convincing cyberman. (And when I say convincing, I mean that the tube wrapped in electrical tape on the cyberman's bionic arm actually fired flaming projectiles that used to be cold capsules!) Jeff's resourcefulness I attribute partly to his father, who's been known to reshape a Ford Pinto fender to fix the trunk of a Mercedes coupe; and to *his* father before him, a university professor and occasional plumber who once claimed that the PhD after his name stood for "Plunge harder, Dad." But most of my son's talent for scrounging comes, I believe, from my father, who died when Jeff was eight.

In 1983, on the last afternoon of my father's life, I said the rosary for him. The idea was not so much to invoke heavenly intercession as to help him fall asleep. I said the rosary as lullaby, the decades droning on and on, one *Hail Mary* after another. My father was very weak by then and it was hard for him to talk, but he finally managed to interrupt.

"I think you're keeping me awake," he whispered.

"Should I sing instead?" I asked him.

He rolled his eyes.

"Sorry," I said.

I would have liked to pick him up and walk him to sleep, the way he used to walk my kids to sleep, cruising around and around our dining room table with Jeff or Liz or Lauren in his arms, singing the same lullaby—half Croatian, half nonsense—that I'd heard him sing to both my little brothers many years ago on 4th Street in Milwaukee. Spavaj sinco moj, lepo spavaj. Sleep, my son, it means. (At least, that's what my father meant by it.) Sleep well, sleep sweetly, beautifully sleep. "Of course it works," my mother liked to say. "They go to sleep so they won't have to listen to your father sing anymore."

There may have been some merit in her theory. My father didn't sing songs; he belted them out. Even lullabies. His favorite tunes were from the forties. At Hofer's Ballroom in Walford, Iowa, I've often surprised my husband on Big Band night by singing the words to "Begin the Beguine" or "Glow Little Glow-Worm" in his ear. Dad also liked beltable songs of a somewhat later era, like "Mac the Knife" and "Hang Down Your Head, Tom Dooley," which gave him goosebumps. "Look at that, look at that," he'd say, interrupting his song to show you the goose-flesh on his arm. "I'm telling you, I missed my calling. I could have made a fortune with this voice."

On 4th Street, there wasn't a kid on the block who would risk raising George Elleseg's ire (and thus his voice) by treading on his front lawn when he was seeding it, which was most of the time, or by taking one of his tools without asking. The tools were in the garage—the same garage that he and two dozen neighbors and a couple of cousins had carried by hand down the alley from its former location behind Butchie Teidemann's house to our yard, where they lowered it gently onto the salvaged brick foundation my father had prepared for it.

Relocated, that garage became the hub of the neighborhood. Your bike had a flat tire? You asked George if you could use his air compressor. You wanted the seat lowered or, as my sister's friend Pat used to say, highered? George was sure to have whatever size wrench you needed. If a screw or a bolt or a nail were required, you peered through the bottoms of dozens of baby food jars whose caps were nailed in rows to the ceiling above his workbench until you found just the size and type you were looking for.

In a neighborhood full of scroungers and do-it-yourselfers, my father was the king. The garage was only one of many accomplishments. Both the stockade fence in our backyard and the privet hedge in front were scrounged—the latter nothing but sticks with roots when Dad picked them out of somebody's garbage cans and planted them along our lot line, deaf to the jokes of neighbors who then watched the sticks grow into a shoulder-high hedge so dense not even the skinniest kid could squeeze through it. Most of the lumber with which he ruined our dark and mysterious attic (by building two nice bedrooms and a walk-in closet) was secondhand and full of silverfish. My sister and I squished torpedo-shaped bugs daily for years.

Like most do-it-yourselfers, my father preferred not to finish a project if he could start a new one instead. With the upstairs lacking only inconsequential details (a bottom track for the closet door to slide on, a handrail for the stairs), my father decided to build a go-cart that resembled a red Model T out of lumber scraps, sheet metal, and that most salvageable of items, an old lawnmower motor. While my little brothers sat up front and steered, my father trotted alongside, ready to hop aboard the rear bumper, flip a switch behind the driver, and drag one foot in the alley until the heavy car rolled to a stop. (The missing detail: brakes.) A few years later, following in my father's footsteps, my brother recycled the wheels and other choice parts of the go-cart to enter a soapbox derby. Later still, when shortness of breath made all my father's tools grow heavier, he and his friend Ralph used two of those same wheels to build a cart for the air compressor.

When it came to recycling, my father was ahead of his time.

After he died, the air compressor went to my soapbox-building brother, which means that Dad's still fixing flat tires in Milwaukee. A lot of his other tools—wrenches and saws, a pipecutter and threader—found their way into our garage and basement, where they have helped us build shelves (and cybermen), fix leaks, and keep a succession of old cars running long after they should have gone to their last reward. They've also taught us a lesson in immortality. Not long ago, in Iowa City, I was sitting on the porch when my husband came outside to pound some stakes in the garden with a hammer from my dad's old workbench. At the top of our porch steps, 265 miles and more than thirty years from the garage on 4th Street, which, by the way, he'd never seen, my husband paused, lifted the wooden handle to the sky, and said, "Just using your hammer, George. Thanks."

HORNET WARS

My Father Strikes Back

JULY 2001

My children are grown up now, but I still feel bad, from time to time, that they were deprived of growing up in my old neighborhood on the south side of Milwaukee, where a real can-do spirit prevailed.

Picture my father, for example, standing in our front yard, girded for battle, his mechanic's overalls rubber-banded at the wrists and stuffed at the ankles into big black boots buckled right up to the top. His neck is swathed in scarves. His hands are double gloved in rubber and suede. Over it all, he wears his black policeman's raincoat. On his head a broad-brimmed hat covered with netting hides his face and disappears into the scarves around his neck. With both gloved hands, he grips the brass nozzle on the end of our green garden hose. The hose snakes around behind him across the lawn to the side of the house, where my mother leans over the spigot, ready to turn on the water when he gives the signal. Crouching in the shadows at the side of our house, she seems to be hiding from the alien being in the front yard.

Stiffly, encumbered by his armor, my father lifts his arm. That's the signal. Water sputters, then shoots in a long, forceful arc from the brass nozzle. It's summer, 1962. The first skirmish in my father's annual war with the hornets is about to begin.

The enemy resides in undetermined numbers in a nest in a pillar on our front porch. My father knows that when it comes to hornets, you can smoke them out or you can flood them out, and being personally acquainted with a man who burned his house to

29

the ground smoking them out, he has chosen water over fire. He twists the nozzle to the off position and clumps up five wooden steps to the porch, dragging the hose behind him. My mother, having done her part, beats a hasty retreat toward the back door. My father is on the front porch now, approaching the pillar stealthily. A hornet or two (I must be imagining these) buzzes in idle curiosity around his broad-brimmed hat and facial netting. My father aims the hose at the dark space where the corner of the porch roof rests on the pillar and twists the nozzle again.

Most of the kids in the neighborhood and a few of their mothers are gathered to watch from a safe distance on Uncle Bud's front lawn, two doors down from our house. From there, we see a white cloud of spray burst into being in the corner of our front porch. My dad stands fast as water glances off the pillar and ceiling. He looks like the captain of a ship in a storm, hauling a crucial line. All at once, the white spray of water turns dark. In Uncle Bud's yard, we take a step or two backward. Hornets pour out of the pillar in impossible quantity. The black cloud of them is mixed up with the water, my dad in the middle of it all.

Suddenly, a cry erupts from the cloud. After the initial expletive, we hear in rapid succession, "Ouch—ouch—ouch—OUCH!" as Dad drops the hose and runs. Straight for Uncle Bud's yard.

The crowd scatters—a disorderly retreat. My friend Judene, who lives in a house across the alley from ours, must not be thinking straight. She tries to make it home through our yard, a mistake that costs her two stings in what we referred to discreetly as her seat.

The hornets fared far worse. When the air cleared, our porch was littered with tiny corpses. My dad must have wiped out a hundred of them. The remaining thousands took up residence for the summer in everyone else's eaves and gutters up and down the block.

When I told this story to my daughter some years ago, she said, not without a certain envy, "You grew up in a weird neighborhood, Mom."

It didn't seem weird at the time, though. Fourth Street between Plainfield and Bolivar was about as ordinary an elm-shaded street as you were likely to find on the south side of Milwaukee. I remember summers passing in sun-speckled boredom. Notable moments—like the water fight that started with Tommy Dragan's squirt gun and ended with my father and his garden hose holding off half the neighborhood, or the time two dozen men lifted Butchie Teidemann's one-and-a-half car garage on the count of three and carried it down the alley to our yard—such moments were few and far between.

"They carried a garage down the alley?" my daughter said. "In their bare hands?"

Not in their bare hands, I told her. They wore their workmen's gloves. Their steel-toed shoes, too, those who had them.

Why, I wondered, would anyone find that odd?

PARADISE LOST

Half a Lesson from Uncle Bud

NOVEMBER 1998

My kids have taken lessons in everything from stage combat to double bass, but in the neighborhood where I grew up, a girl had only two choices: accordion lessons or baton. Pam Dragan and I took baton. Once a week, we walked five blocks under a canopy of elms from 4th Street to Howell Avenue, where our teacher lived, brandishing our batons, indulging now and then in a march step or two, toes pointed, knees raised high. We shared our half-hour lesson with two chubby little girls—sisters—who, if memory serves me correctly, always wore their sequin-spangled leotards. Probably they only wore these outfits once in a while, but that's how I remember them, dressed for success. My friend Pam and I wore cotton-print Jamaica shorts that came with matching sleeveless blouses. Our mothers bought us three or four of these short sets at the start of each summer. After a couple of weeks, I'd be wearing the yellow plaid shorts with the red, white, and blue sailboat top, setting up a rotation that left me mismatched for the rest of the season.

We practiced our baton twirling in Pam's backyard for at least one half hour a day, no matter how bruised our elbows got. Unlike the sparkling sisters, Pam and I never twirled in a single parade, but we had our private moments of glory. There were times, for example, when we managed to do the horizontal over-and-under twirl at high speed, not once banging our elbows with our batons, which, on the count of three, we threw into the air *together* and then stood our ground without flinching, keeping our eyes on those batons as they went up like propellers flashing silver against the evening sky.

Sometimes we even caught them on their way back down.

When we did, we were often rewarded with applause from Uncle Bud, who lived next door to the Dragans and spent his summer evenings watering his garden or sitting on his back porch, smoke curling away from his pipe like a little gray banner.

We didn't know what to make of Uncle Bud—a bachelor, living alone on 4th Street, his house the only Lannon stone ranch in a two-block stretch of wooden frame houses and Milwaukee bungalows. He was a guy our fathers' age with a round face, a salt-and-pepper crew cut, and a pipe stem always clenched between his teeth. We tried to imagine why he wasn't married, proposing various tragedies that might have robbed him of wife and kids and the chance for a normal life. Jealously we wondered what he did with the two spare bedrooms in his three-bedroom ranch. But most of all, we vied for the privilege of running down to the corner store for him, to pick up a can of shaving cream or a loaf of bread and keep the change.

Uncle Bud sent me to the store only once—an occasion I remember decades later in painfully sharp detail. One bright evening, when I was balancing my baton on my index finger in Pam's yard, waiting for her to come outside, I heard Uncle Bud whistle from his back porch. He waved me over. He was all out of half-n-half, he told me when I reached his porch steps. Could I run to the store for him? "Just get a small one," he said, and dropping a musical handful of quarters into my palm, he added the words I was waiting for: "Keep the change."

When I got back from the store, Uncle Bud was nowhere in sight, so I rang the bell and waited, my Popsicle dripping, my licorice ropes getting stickier by the minute, and a wax carton of half-n-half sweating in the crook of my arm. I rang the bell again. From somewhere inside the house Uncle Bud hollered, "Who is it?" and I yelled through the screen, "It's me."

"Who?"

"With the half-n-half."

A pause followed, then the muffled voice again: "Put it on the counter."

I transferred the licorice ropes and Popsicle to the hand that held the half-n-half, wiped my fingers on my Jamaica shorts (sailboats today), and pulled the handle on the screen door. Inside, the house had what I thought of for years afterward as a bachelor smell: a blend of pipe tobacco, aftershave, mothballs, furniture wax, and Airwick room deodorizer. I took a deep breath of it, crossed the shining kitchen floor, set the carton on the counter, and scooted out the back door again.

I had gone but a few steps from the house when I heard the squeak of hinges behind me, followed by a quizzical "Hey!" I turned around. Uncle Bud was standing in the doorway with the one-pint carton of half-n-half in his hand.

"What's this?" he said.

It was like a trick question. I said, "Half-n-half."

He stood there, looking at the carton as if it were an artifact from another world, which, in a way, it was. Finally, I had to ask, "Is something wrong?"

He said, "I was hoping for tobacco."

For a split second I thought he'd answered me in Arabic or something. Then I got it. Tobacco. Uncle Bud was hoping for *tobacco*. I could picture packages of it behind the counter at the corner store, above the rows of cigarettes. Half-n-Half Burly & Bright ("A Cargo of Contentment in the Bowl of Any Pipe") was right there on the shelf, in a green and red package between boxes of Captain Black and cans of Prince Albert. I had *seen* the tobacco. I had thought, "Do you have Prince Albert in a can? Well, let him out!" And then I had purchased a Popsicle, two licorice ropes, and a one-pint carton of the kind of half-n-half my mother would have sent me for.

The ground did not open and swallow me up in Uncle Bud's

yard; it never does when you need it to. I had to run all the way back to my house and hide in the basement instead. We had a dungeon of a basement on 4th Street—wooden joists and heating ducts to bang your head on, dripping pipes, an old converted octopus furnace in the middle of it all. I stood down there in the former coal bin, watching tears of humiliation darken the dust on my tennis shoes and remembering Uncle Bud's chuckle. I looked down at my yellow plaid blouse and my red, white, and blue sailboat shorts. Like Eve discovering her nakedness, I saw for the first time how dumb I looked.

OLD COUNTRY,
NEW COUNTRY

WHAT'S IN A NAME

The Ellis Eggs

FEBRUARY 1999

Pethe ople ask me about my name. Stefaniak. Is it Czech? Is it Polish? It's Polish, but it's not my name. My husband is the Stefaniak, at least on his father's side.

What about me, then? What's *my* name?

What people mean, of course, is what's my father's name. Nobody wonders why I'm not a McCullough like my mother, whose name I coveted as a child, especially on St. Patrick's Day, not knowing it was "Scotch-Irish" and not much to do with St. Patrick. But even if we overlook issues of gender and patriarchy, my name has a complicated story.

It starts with my father's parents, born in the 1880s in a Croatian village that ended up in Hungary after the First World War. (Most of the rest of Croatia ended up in the Kingdom of the Serbs, Croats, and Slovenes for a while, and then, for a longer while, in Yugoslavia.) After the war, the village school switched from Croatian to Hungarian, and to this day, if you ask my relatives in Old World or New about their nationality, they'll tell you they're Hungarian—although everybody, including my American-born father, spoke Croatian, and many of them, like my cousin Marie Sinyakovich, still have their Croatian names.

In Hungarian, my family name is Iliasics. If you spell it in Croatian, it looks quite different—letters changing and little accent marks sprouting here and there—but either way you spell it, it's pronounced the same, roughly: eel-YA-shich. The name I grew up with, on the other hand, sounds like this: "Ellis egg." I was Mary Helen Elleseg. Elsie, in some quarters, for short.

One of your more obvious Ellis Island christenings, Elleseg is a name my grandfather acquired upon coming to America. Unless you live in Spokane, Washington, or near Milwaukee, Wisconsin, you probably won't find it in your phone book. You will find it on a half-dozen gravestones (there are, to my knowledge, precisely six dead Ellesegs in the world today) and on family documents going back to at least 1923, the year my father was born in Milwaukee. Before that, on naturalization papers, for example, some confusing variation occurs.

I've known about my two names—both Old Country and Ellis Island versions—for as long as I can remember, although I learned only recently about differences in Hungarian and Croatian phonetics. For years, I'd figured my relatives didn't know how to spell. As it turns out, they knew how to spell in two languages. (When they learned English, they made it three.)

I was in sixth grade when I wrote the saga of my grandmother's first coming to America, a journey she undertook to join my grandfather, who was already here. She came in 1910, with fifty dollars and their five-year-old daughter, Madeline. In an interview taped in 1985, my Aunt Madeline still remembered how the immigration inspector had marked her little black coat with a big white X and sent her into the line on the left, while my grandmother was sent to the right. Poor Grandma wailed and cried and fought to get to her daughter while officials tried explaining to her in several languages (not including Hungarian or Croatian) that Aunt Madeline had the measles.

After some time (weeks, it seemed to Aunt Madeline) in quarantine, they continued their journey to Milwaukee, my hometown, a place my grandmother disliked so much that three years later, in June 1913, she was on another boat heading back to the Old Country, this time with eight-year-old Madeline and a toddler (my Uncle Joe). The Great War intervened, and the three of them remained in the village until 1921, when my grandfather threatened to stop sending money from America if his wife and kids didn't come home.

Home? my grandmother must have thought.

Like my family, our ancestral village also has two different names. In Hungarian it's Tótújfalu; in Croatian, Novo Selo, which means New Village, although the village has stood beside the Drava River, now part of the Hungarian-Croatian border, for five hundred years.

In 1994, I went to Hungary with my seventy-five-year-old cousin Marie Sinyakovich to see the village, which is Marie's hometown, for myself. In many ways it was like visiting relatives anywhere. People took me here, they took me there. This one kissed me, that one kissed me, everyone kissed me. A childhood friend of my cousin clasped her hands together, her eyes swimming behind coke-bottle glasses, and called me "Lepa moja." My pretty one.

In the village of my grandparents' birth—where cows taken out to pasture in the morning still came home at dusk on the dirt road with their cowherd behind them, occasionally causing trouble for the evening bus from Szigetvár—I walked around in a continuous state of déjà vu.

Everywhere I looked I saw my Aunt Madeline—her babushka, her apron, her bun. Everything that had made Aunt Madeline's yard a little odd on Walker Street in Milwaukee was typical here: the grapevines, the plank paths through the garden, the flowers mixed up with the vegetables, the Blessed Virgin enshrined on a stick in the middle of it all. Everything well tended but not too neat, not too rigidly classified. Bleeding hearts among the roses.

Amazing things happened to me in that village. I got treed by a pig picking cherries in my cousin's yard. (I was the one picking cherries.) I rode a bicycle along the Drava River in the shade of trees planted sixty-five years ago by the schoolchildren of Novo Selo, my traveling companion Marie among them.

People I'd never seen before looked so familiar—here an older version of my cousin Johnny, there a younger version of my brother George. They invited me into their homes, little houses with foot-thick walls, embroidered panels hung to hide the dampness. They fed me fry cakes and palačinkas made from the same unwritten recipes that my Aunt Madeline used and that my grandmother used before her.

Relatives I'd never heard of showed me photographs that Grandma and Aunt Madeline had sent them over the years. They had a snapshot of *me* at age five with my policeman father looming behind me, his hands just reaching my shoulders, my grin a copy of his. They had me at thirteen, posing at the Milwaukee airport with a visiting cousin from the village, who was dressed up for travel in a suit and sandals. They had me at age seventeen, a bridesmaid at my sister's wedding. There I was, there we all were, my brothers and their go-kart, my sister dolled up for prom, our house in Milwaukee, all of it in boxes marked with words I couldn't read.

Who says you can never go home again? You can—even if you've never been there before.

PHOTO OPPORTUNITIES

Memory Takes a Better Picture

NOVEMBER 1999

I 'm the kind of person who routinely misses photo opportunities. When my son—my firstborn—graduated from high school, I didn't even manage to get a cap-and-gown shot with the family, including grandparents who had traveled some distance to be there. Before I knew what was what, Jeff had exchanged his gown for his diploma, and everybody was looking for lunch. I grieved for a long time over the once-in-a-lifetime opportunity we had missed.

When I went to Hungary with my father's cousin Marie Sinyakovich in 1994, I was determined not to make the same mistake. I took so many pictures of the ancestral village that she made fun of me for whipping out the camera every thirty seconds. I took pictures of houses (including the one where cousin Marie was born), of grapevine-covered hillsides, and of the four-hundred-year-old village church. I took pictures of pigs and red brick barns and of a kind of well you could find in every yard—an ancient design with a bucket on a pole suspended from one end of a tree trunk that was balanced like a seesaw in the crook of another tree trunk. (Here's where I wish I could say, "See photo.")

So maybe I did take too many pictures of cows coming home down the village street, each one turning off into her yard like so many cars pulling into their driveways. ("Until the cows come home" means something very specific to me now.) And I certainly took more pictures than I needed of storks' nests on chimney tops and light poles. But I also took pictures worth more than a thousand words apiece: Marie and an old school friend with their arms around each other's waists, Marie white-haired and apple-cheeked, her friend in babushka and apron. My father's cousin Paul Bunyevacz beside his bicycle on the banks of the Drava River, the wide water behind him and the identical leafy landscape of Croatia on the other side. And what about the cowherd who went door to door each morning, downing a shot glass of plum brandy in each customer's kitchen? For Christmas that year, I gave Marie a twelve-by-fourteen of that cowherd following his charges down the road, his whip in his hand and his dog at his heels. She framed it and hung it in her living room.

I missed no photo opportunities on that trip, believe me, and when I came home I put all the keepers in a photo album (this was in the predigital days of negatives and prints), arranging them by place and time and adding a roadmap of Hungary with our little village and other spots circled in red. I toted that album around all summer, showing it to everybody.

Until I lost it. I might have left it in a booth at a restaurant in Milwaukee. The negatives? I have them. Somewhere.

Luckily, Marie Sinyakovich and I went back to Hungary five summers later, this time with my daughter Lauren, fresh out of high school (having been duly photographed with cap, gown, and family members), and my sister Sandra, owner of a spiffy camera that we kept leaving in panoramic mode, accidentally cutting off the heads of our nonpanoramic relatives. We got the essential shots, though: cows, storks, wells, and more.

Our itinerary was about the same as the previous trip. After a night in Budapest, we were off to Marie's sister Agnes in Pécs, a medium-sized city in the south that offers Turkish and Roman ruins, a thousand-year-old church, and mountainous terrain to remind you that you're just north of the Balkans. (All this *and* Agnes's homemade cabbage strudel!) From Pécs we went to the tiny village of Tótszentgyörgy (a fully pronounceable, entirely phonetic word, by the way). There we stayed with Marie's sister Ann and her husband, Kalman. I was sad to learn they'd sold their cow, so the cowherd no longer stopped by for his morning pick-me-up.

"Good thing you got that picture of him last time," Marie said. "The one I got on my wall."

Our next stop was the ancestral village itself, Tótújfalu in Hungarian, Novo Selo in Croatian, where we took another round of pictures of the same places and relatives I'd snapped and lost—getting all the babies and toddlers who weren't around five years earlier, some with heads and some without. The sight of my father's cousin Paul Bunyevacz, now eighty and looking as if his bicycling days were over, reminded me sharply of the picture whose loss I mourned the most.

It was taken the day Paul and I had bicycled down the road along the Drava. Before we set off, we posed in the yard for a picture that I can close my eyes right now and see, down to the last detail: I'm in jeans, a T-shirt, and the white, white sweater that Marie's sister had washed so carefully for me by hand. Paul wears baggy denim dungarees rolled up to clear the tops of his sandals, a one-button sport coat, and a brown sweater vest over a gold shirt buttoned all the way up to the neck. A well-seasoned golf cap slouches on his head. Under the cap he has great bushy eyebrows, blue eyes like our mutual cousin Marie, a hawkish nose, and thick white hair that falls forward in a shock of bangs like the early Beatles. He looks younger than seventy-five in the picture I remember, holding up his bicycle next to mine, with a red brick barn and baby turkeys in the background. He looks as vigorous and firmly planted as the cherry trees behind him.

"Too bad I lost that great picture Marie took of us with the bikes," I said—or tried to. My Croatian is hit or miss. Mostly miss.

"This one?" Paul asked me, holding his scrapbook open to the page where he'd pasted the reprint I sent him. He handed it over and I took a look.

I was shocked. This picture was not a thing like the one I

remembered. This picture was about the scraggly grass and brown tire tracks in the foreground, instead of the two bicyclists posing a third of the way up the frame. There were no cherry trees in it, no baby turkeys either. The red brick barn looked tumble-down instead of charming. As for Paul and me, my sweater was white, but I looked fat and blurry of face, and he was wearing brown oxfords—far more practical than the sandals and socks I remembered. His hair was combed back, and his shirt opened at the neck (it was June after all), not buttoned all the way up like a little boy's. The golf cap dangled from the handlebars.

Looking at my face as I looked at the photo, Paul raised a bushy eyebrow and clapped me on the shoulder. He said some-thing. I didn't get it. He tried again, first tapping one finger to his temple, then holding thumbs and index fingers as if to aim a camera, and this time I understood: "Memory takes a better picture."

Of course it does. I thought of my son marching up the aisle in his green graduation gown, his face looking long and lean under the silly green mortar board, his head shaved on the sides (in ful-fillment of an oath sworn by his four-by-four team if they made it to State), his face and neck almost delicate in their nakedness—the way those very young Marines in the Few Good Men posters always look more vulnerable than grim. He looks, I think, like my father, who died long before Jeff was old enough for us to see how strong the resemblance would be. My father had the same angular face and frowning eyes. At least, that's the way I remem-ber him.

NOW THERE IS A MIRACLE,
AND DON'T MATTER WHAT

DECEMBER 2003

T ake the time my grandmother gave her last fifty dollars
to another poor woman, who was pulling out her own
hair on the boat to America while her children wailed
around her. It was 1921. Traveling with my grandmother were her
sixteen-year-old daughter (Aunt Madeline) and her eight-year-
old son (Uncle Joe). They were coming from their village in Hungary to rejoin my grandfather in Milwaukee after a seven-year
separation occasioned by the First World War.

The woman who was pulling out her hair didn't know you had
to have fifty dollars in your pocket when you got off the boat in
New York. "Oh, yoy!" the woman had been crying, "I don't have
no money. That's why we're going to America!" My grandmother
knew that she could wire my grandfather in Milwaukee to send
her fifty dollars, so she went ahead and gave the money to her
desperate fellow passenger.

"Now there is a miracle, and don't matter what," Aunt Madeline used to say every time she told me this story. "Because we
gotta wait for that money to come, we don't get on the train right
away from New York to Chicago. And next day we find out that
train got in a big wreck and lotsa people killed. That's in 1921, you
can look it up. If my ma didn't give that money away, we woulda
been on that train."

"So did the woman and her kids get killed?" I had to ask.

"What? No, no. That was the train to Chicago, and they was
going someplace else."

My aunt was fluent—though not always standard—in English, Hungarian, and Croatian. When I mentioned this to a

linguist at a university reception years ago, he seemed to regard it as a kind of miracle. He explained that these three languages belong to three great language families, which operate in three entirely different ways. After a bit more chat about inflection and accretion and who knows what, the linguist, small plate of hors d'oeuvres in hand, asked me, "And what does your linguistically talented aunt do for a living?"

I told him she worked in a bank, which was true. She was a cleaning lady for many years at First American in Milwaukee.

Another miracle, this one in Iowa City.

My husband and I were walking down Gilbert Street one winter night, arms linked and hands stuffed in our respective pockets, on our way to the new Korean restaurant. A car went by, kids hooting, and something hit John in the back. We both whirled around to see, our arms disengaging. "Ow," said John. "What was that?" I'd seen a white flash so we thought maybe a snowball, although the back of John's coat was dry. We shrugged it off and went across the street into the restaurant.

After dinner (bok choi, bulgogi), I stood up, put on my coat, and slipped my hands into the pockets, looking for gloves. I stopped.

"John," I said. "There's something in my pocket."

He asked what, of course, but I couldn't quite say. I was still rolling it around in there.

"I think it's an egg."

"You mean like a ceramic egg?" We had a couple of those at home.

"No," I said. "A real one." And I drew it out, whole and white, from my coat pocket.

"How did it get in there?" he said.

The miraculous truth was not the first thing that occurred to us. "Maybe it's from the restaurant?" I said. It had opened only recently. "Maybe the waitress slips an egg in your pocket and you win a year's supply of bulgogi."

There was no such grand-opening deal. We were the victims, or in this case, the beneficiaries, of an egging! We had to talk ourselves into believing how it must have happened. The raw egg that hit John squarely in the back had not only failed to break but had somehow rolled down the arm of my black coat—the flash of white—and into my pocket, guided into it like a foot guided into a shoe by a shoehorn, at the very instant when I pulled my hand out.

Miracle Number Three, I'd say. Or Four. (Who's counting?)

Just before Christmas my son calls from Florida. He's twenty-seven.

(That's a miracle right there: How could my son be twenty-seven?) He says, "Hey, Mom. You know how I never do anything in the traditional way?"

I hear in his words, in the tone of his voice, the way he announced the frog pond that he and the girls dug in the yard one spring and lined with plastic garbage bags. I hear the faint echo of his blessedly brief but consuming interest in pyrotechnics, remembering scores of packages of tiny firecrackers he gutted for their fuses and grains of gunpowder. I picture him with the radio-controlled car he transformed by means of spray paint and cardboard into K-9, the robot dog from *Doctor Who*. I see him in a Halloween costume constructed of foam packaging materials and circuit boards ingeniously attached to a zip-front jumpsuit that I actually wore in the 1970s, oblivious, at the time, to the robot within.

"Yes?" I say into the phone (aware for only an instant of the miracle that makes him sound so near).

From a thousand miles away, my son says, "Well, I got married!"

My husband and I had to wait until June to spend a few days with our son and his new wife in Florida. Monika was waiting for us at the hotel, wearing the polo shirt that my husband's sister had sent her from the family real estate office in Milwaukee, the one with "The Stefaniak Group" embroidered on the pocket. I don't know exactly what it was about her—the way she sort of danced into the shy hug she gave me, or the way she kept taking Jeff's arm, or maybe it was the wholehearted way she played *Pictionary* with us one afternoon, although English is not her first language. Something told me almost at once that my son had found someone who loves him at least as much as I do.

And what was it about Jeff? He seemed different, closer to us somehow. It was as if all those barriers we construct to protect ourselves against the slings and arrows of growing up were suddenly unnecessary for him to maintain, as if opening the door to let Monika in had opened a door for the rest of us too.

And if all that is not miracle enough for you, consider this: Monika is from Hungary. When they go to visit her parents next summer, she can take Jeff to see the village my grandmother left in 1921.

We know what Aunt Madeline would say about that.

THEORIES
OF THE SELF

THE RIGHT CLOTHES

Finding Yourself in the Fitting Room

OCTOBER 1998

I can't get over the feeling that my life would be different—better, of course—if only I had the right clothes. This feeling makes me buy things I don't need at sidewalk sales. It makes me waste my time poring over catalogs, ordering things and sending them back, ostensibly because they don't fit but really because they don't make me look like the model in the catalog. Among the reasons for return on the form, I almost always choose "Not as pictured."

The problem is partly fiscal. I don't have the resources to stroll into Ann Taylor or Von Maur (much less Gucci or Prada) and pluck from the racks whatever strikes my fancy. "Tell me about it," says my daughter Liz. For a while, her idea of the right clothes was a wardrobe of tailored suits like the ones Scully wears on *The X-Files*. "Do you know how much it would cost to dress like that?" Liz says. "And the dry cleaning?!"

For people like Liz and me, with limited budgets but lofty sartorial ambitions, resale shops offer unique and affordable opportunities to find the right clothes. Added to the thrill of a good bargain, in a resale shop you get the endorsement of the original owner, who paid full price, and when, against all odds, you find something that fits you, there is a sense of rightness, of destiny fulfilled.

Take the prom dress Liz found at the Savvy Boutique. It was an elegant jade green sheath: knee-length, short-sleeved, close-fitting, and completely covered with dime-sized green sequins. When Liz came out of the fitting room in the dress, which fit and shimmered on her like a mermaid's tail, the sequins rippling like scales, the saleswoman said, "Oh my! Doesn't that dress say, *Party! Party! Party!*"

Liz considered herself in the mirror. "To me," she mused, "it says—*fish.*"

Liz was a sensation in her fish dress at prom. Every time she moved, the sequins produced a rushing sound, like gently breaking waves or well-deserved applause.

Some people have an unerring instinct for the right clothes. Liz is one, and my friend Leslee is another. When Leslee was in town last July for the Summer Writing Festival, we met downtown and walked to Vito's for dinner. Vito's happened to be next door to the Hall Mall, then home to a newly opened vintage clothing store called Fat Tulip. Leslee and I paused between the two doors—one leading to food, the other to clothes. We took note of Fat Tulip's business hours. We glanced at our watches. "It's still open," we both said.

Twenty minutes later, we emerged, hungry as bears, Leslee the new owner of a gray canvas workman's jacket with a grain elevator and the words "Felco Farmer's Coop, Conroy, Iowa" embroidered on the back. I had acquired a sleeveless pink Ship 'n Shore blouse with a prim little Peter Pan collar and buttons down the front. When I wore the blouse—once—with black capris, I was a dead ringer for Laura Petrie on the old *Dick Van Dyke Show.* (Remember Mary Tyler Moore as the wife with the warbly voice and the toreador pants?) Leslee, on the other hand, looked like a rural rebel without a cause in her Felco Farmer jacket.

But I've had my share of success. In a consignment shop in Denver, I once found a navy-blue suit with a broad-shouldered, waist-cinching jacket and calf-length skirt that was nothing less than stunning, right down to the covered buttons on the kick-pleat. I was already inclined to follow the first rule of resale shopping ("If the suit fits, buy it!"), when I looked in the fitting room mirror and saw someone who looked as cool and sultry as Lauren

Bacall gazing back at me. (I refer, of course, to the Golden-Age-of-Hollywood star who tells Humphrey Bogart how to whistle in *To Have and Have Not*: "Just put your lips together and blow.") The sale was made. Writing up the receipt, the shop owner told me that she herself had worn this very suit to small claims court in a recent dispute with her landlord.

"Did you win?" I asked her.

"Of course," she said.

I don't know why I even asked. My Lauren Bacall suit is not the sort of thing that a loser would wear. Whoever bought it years ago knew what she was doing. When I wear it, I like to imagine that a little of her savvy rubs off on me.

That's what the right clothes, new or vintage, are really all about. Whether we're hastily undressing in a curtained corner at Secondhand Rose or piling up designer outfits in a plush fitting room, we're not just trying on clothes. We're trying on possibilities. We're seeing who and what we might be. (Except, of course, when we try on swimsuits. Trying on swimsuits, we're seeing who we cannot be. Not anymore. No sir.)

Recently, in a resale shop in Milledgeville, Georgia, home of famous author Flannery O'Connor, I made my mother, my aunt, my sister, and my daughter wait for me while I tried on fifteen dresses, not one of which fit. I suppose I was hoping that a little "famous author" would rub off on me if I wore something once worn by someone walking down the same streets O'Connor once did.

My mother is also from Milledgeville. In fact, the resale shop was only half a block from the old USO where she and her sisters used to dance with lonely servicemen when they were teenagers during the Second World War. After I gave up on finding a dress, my mother gave us a tour. She showed us the corner drugstore where they used to buy sodas and the building that used to be Peabody High—her alma mater and the famous author's.

Then my mother told us a story that just goes to show how

clothes can shape your destiny. We already knew that she'd met my father when he was stationed in Georgia—a young man so keenly aware that his Army Air Corps uniform was the right clothes that he used to stand the whole way on the bus into town to save the crease in his pants. We also knew that on the fateful night when she'd accidentally made dates to meet two different guys at the USO at the same time, Dad and his sharp creases had won out over the local flyboy who'd been pursuing her. What we didn't know was that the local flyboy, now a handsome officer, had asked her to come down to Texas for his graduation. She would have gone—and perhaps erased our family history—but she couldn't, she said.

Why not? we asked her.

"I didn't have anything to wear."

ARE WE REALLY WORTH IT?

On Coloring One's Hair

DECEMBER 2000

I do it myself, standing in front of the bathroom mirror, wearing a tattered T-shirt hand-decorated with literary quotes and characters from my son's Advanced Placement English class. The face of Kurtz stares into the mirror from the *Heart of Darkness* in the middle of my chest, his already ghoulish fabric-paint features stained anew with L'Oréal Excellence Color Creme.

"The horror! The horror!" he cries.

It's not so bad, really, thirty minutes' worth of standing around with goop that smells like permanent wave solution glopped all over your head. You have a cup of coffee, careful not to let your head touch any fabric or other porous surfaces on the way down to the kitchen, you watch the goop go from white to brown, and you rinse it out.

I use No. 5G—Medium Golden Brown—which, on me, is dark brown tending to red and not in the least golden, but it's better than the lighter browns, which go a little green in certain kinds of light if you're a swimmer.

Like most home beauty products, the instructions are complex, fraught with warnings, and long enough in English and Spanish to fill two sides of a twelve-by-twelve-inch sheet. Fortunately, after two or three uses of the product, the instructions, like most instructions, can be ignored. I reread them once in a while to make sure they haven't put something new and startling in there, like *Product may be hazardous when applied by left-handed persons of Eastern European descent* or *Don't try this at home.*

But a word of caution. Lest I lead prospective users of hair color products down the path to hair breakage, unforeseen color results, or worse, let me officially recommend a careful perusal of the instruction sheet before first use — particularly the five column inches of "IMPORTANT INFORMATION ABOUT HAIR COLOR." Here we find out that we must

> *Keep hair coloring products out of the reach of children* (duh); *Use only plastic or glass utensils — never metal —* for reasons that are not explained and thus make us worry about unimaginable similarities between home hair color and the microwave oven; *Take care not to leave the applicator tip unopened after mixing and do not save it once it has been mixed because to do so may cause container to burst*; and, finally, *Immediately rinse with cool water if mixture accidentally gets into eyes, call a doctor if irritation persists, and never use hair color on eyelashes or eyebrows. To do so may cause blindness.*

Once, in the locker room at the Iowa City rec center, I came upon a young woman with a towel wrapped around her torso and her gooped-up hair piled loosely on top of her head. By its distinctive smell, I recognized the non-drip revitalizing color creme, which, to my horror, the young woman had also applied to her eyebrows, the darkened smear over each eye giving her a Groucho Marx look. She was sitting on a bench, passing the thirty minutes of color developing time (thirty-five for resistant grays) by reading a paperback, apparently oblivious to the fact that it might be the last paperback she would ever read. I almost called 911.

I have no illusions about why I color my hair. It's not for the "resiliency and new body" promised on the box, not even for the "rich color." It's certainly not "because *I'm worth it*." Like everyone my age who uses the stuff, it's "maximum gray coverage" I'm after.

When I first started coloring my hair, I kept it a secret from everyone, even my family. Oh, it was a furtive little business, wrapping up the dirty plastic gloves and the stained T-shirts and taking them right out to the trash. One time, when tiny holes in the gloves left my fingers Medium Brown for a week, I told people that my hands were stained from picking up walnuts in our yard. (I considered telling them it was wood stain from a furniture refinishing project, but I decided to go with the walnuts.)

I'm not sure why I needed to keep my hair coloring secret. Maybe it was the legacy of coming of age in the early '70s, when beauty had to be "natural" or it didn't count. Whatever you looked like, you had to look as if you were born that way—with that blush across your cheeks, those long black lashes, the stick-straight Cher hair. (Starving yourself for a stick-straight body was okay, though; starving, after all, is a natural process.)

I have made some progress over the years. Now, instead of hiding from him, I ask my husband to put on his glasses and help me spot any hard-to-catch drips on the back of my neck and ears. Last week, when I walked into the classroom and a student asked me if there was something different about my hair, I told him boldly, "It's darker."

The other day, I overheard a conversation between a shop owner, her hair a tell-tale reddish brown, and a customer whose gray and white hair was swept up in a loose French twist. "I found out that the money I spent on my hair would pay for a teacher in Honduras," the gray-haired customer said. "Now there's another teacher in Honduras." Since I buy only one box of L'Oréal Excellence every six weeks—often with a seventy-five-cents-off coupon—the money I spend on my hair color probably wouldn't buy a teacher in Honduras much more than a year's supply of pencils. Still, that's a lot of pencils.

I'm not quite ready to let my hair go au naturel, but I have charged my daughters with the responsibility of informing me when my skin is so wrinkled and my overall appearance so aged that I look silly with Medium Golden Brown hair. I'm kind of looking forward to the day. "Getting old isn't so bad," my father used to say, "when you consider the alternative."

TAKE ME OUT TO THE BALL GAME

I Don't Care If I *Ever* Get Back. Really I Don't.

SEPTEMBER 2012

I've been watching a lot of baseball lately—these past few seasons, I mean. I'm not sure why. I don't root for a particular team, although I have my favorite players. Not that I need a fancy reason to enjoy the Great American Pastime. But why did I spend most of my life feeling that professional baseball was the most boring of spectator sports (well, the second most, after golf) whereas now I find every pitch—*every* pitch—absolutely gripping?

"Did you say '*gripping*'?" my sister-in-law asked me recently.

"Yes!" I said.

She said, "Hunh."

Some of it has to do with camera angles. You don't have to be a Phillies fan to appreciate a close-up of Cliff Lee's Gary-Cooperesque face while he squints with fierce determination from the pitcher's mound, and you don't have to know the Cubs from the White Sox (believe me) to feel your heart go out to young Starlin Castro biting his lip at the plate (before he smashes one out of the park). As currently televised—whether at home or on the giant video screens at the ballparks—baseball offers more convincing emotion, play by play, than reruns of *Law and Order*.

It's the ultimate reality TV. These guys are *intense*. They're not playacting. You can tell by the way they chew and spit and adjust their underwear in public. And consider the umpires, especially the ones behind home plate. Would they straighten their Frankenstein shoulders and stand by their most outrageous calls if they had a chance to do another take? When they get it wrong—calling a strike a ball, or vice versa, thus sealing the fate of the pitcher or turning the batter's good "take" into a strike-out—there's nothing they or anyone else can do about it. The damage is done.

They're like book reviewers that way.

In one sense, baseball and I go way back. At St. Veronica's Grade School in Milwaukee, our principal, a stately nun of the Order of St. Francis, was an ardent fan of the *Milwaukee* Braves. (I did say "way back.") Thanks to Sister Ignatius, O.S.F., we heard the Braves beat the Yankees over the school's public address system in 1957, fifty of us first graders sitting in long, straight rows of desks that must have looked about as infinite as any first-base line to the poor teacher up front. We even *watched* a World Series game one time, on a television usually reserved for our weekly dose of Sister Tomasita's *Let's Make Art!*, which came to us live from Cardinal Stritch College on the other side of town.

Our school was near the airport. The nuns took every opportunity to march us up to Howell Avenue, where we waved at motorcades of notables on their way downtown from General Mitchell Field. Even if I'm not quite sure that I *remember* the convertibles full of World Champion Milwaukee Braves rolling past in 1957, I was *there*, a first grader on tiptoe at the curb, waving with a host of others at Henry Aaron and Eddie Mathews and Warren Spahn.

An experience like that probably marks a person for life, whether she knows it or not. We're talking about a little girl who spent her formative years thinking that the last line in the national anthem went "O'er the land of the free and the home of the Braves." Why else did they sing it at baseball games?

All of that went underground for me when the Braves left Milwaukee. I hardly noticed the arrival of the Brewers in—well, I'd have to look up the date. I might not have noticed them at all if it hadn't been for George Webb restaurants changing their billboard-sized signs that used to predict the Milwaukee Braves would win twelve games straight in whatever season was currently in progress. It was the Milwaukee Brewers, not the Braves, who finally made George Webb's home team prediction come true, resulting in an all-day giveaway of miniburgers, but that was after I left Milwaukee for Iowa in 1982. The Brewers made the World Series that fall. I didn't watch a single game.

Others have written more eloquently and knowledgeably than I ever could about the many analogies to be drawn between baseball—with its emphasis on coming home and how hard it can be to get there—and life, so I won't spend my word count there. I'm just trying to figure out why it suddenly means so much to me that Cliff Lee pitched ten strikeouts in the first game of the 2009 World Series, that he allowed the Yankees no earned runs in the whole game, and that, when one of them managed to hit a line drive straight at the pitcher's mound, Lee spun around and caught that ball *behind his back*.

Why do I pity anyone who missed the 2011 series game in which the Cardinals got to the point of what would have been their last out *twice*—and then went on to win in the eleventh inning with a walk-off homer by St. Louis hometown boy David Freese?

In *A Great and Glorious Game*, A. Bartlett Giamatti reminds us that in baseball, time doesn't matter. Like a lot of people, I used to hold that against the game—but no more. The last time I was at Yankee Stadium, I could hardly believe my good fortune when the ninth inning ended at 0-0, as did the tenth. Even a nine-inning game can be stretched out by fouls and walks and singles. I love the way the count can be 3 and 2, with two outs, bases loaded (or not), and still the at-bat can go on and on—"Way to get a piece of it!"—forever.

Does it have to do with getting, as they say, older? Is that why scoreless innings that would have made me fidget as a kid now keep me at the edge of my seat? Or am I drawn to the impossible odds of the batter stepping up to the plate, one guy against nine, taking his stance while everyone thinks, *Hunh*, let's see what *you* can do. And if the batter's box is a lonely spot, how much lonelier is the pitcher's mound? Sure, the pitcher's got his team in the field behind him and the catcher signaling him from up front, but nobody's looking at the catcher or the fielders. All eyes are on the pitcher, the game suspended like a breath until he throws a ball or a strike or maybe allows a hit that makes the whole field spring into action like a pinball machine. In the stands, crowds big enough to populate small cities leap as one to their feet.

Back in May, I heard a sportscaster talking about Albert Pujols, who's hitting—or not hitting, at least back in May—for the Angels this year, instead of St. Louis. (This is 2012, remember.) The announcer said Pujols was looking at where we were in the season and asking himself if he still had time to come up with the numbers. (As it turns out, he did. A Los Angeles Dodger in 2021, he's well past three thousand hits and counting.)

I often ask myself if I still have time to come up with the numbers. Being a writer, I'm looking for pages, rather than hits or runs, but it just goes to show that we have something in common, Pujols and I. That, and our love of a game where time doesn't matter.

Plus, our salaries.

I mean, we both get one.

EXERCISING
OPTIONS

THE PORRIDGE CLUB

"First We Swim. Then We Eat."

FEBRUARY 1998

Between the ages of sixteen, when I completed my two years of required physical education at St. Mary's Academy, and forty, when I'd told myself it was time to get my rear in gear at last, I had no regular exercise program. I had three kids in those years—which meant plenty of running, chasing, and weightlifting daily—and in my midtwenties I trained briefly for a five-mile benefit run that I completed in just under an hour, collecting my pledges on eleven-minute miles that almost ruined my knees for good. I also dabbled in racquetball and danced in the living room from time to time. Ask my grown daughters if they recall doing Jane Fonda's Workout with Mom—also in the living room—to the beat of Michael Jackson's "Thriller." Torturous positions like The Plow are no problem, by the way, for three- and five-year-olds.

I must have been about thirty-five, with my youngest still a preschooler, when I made my vow to exercise at forty, an age I then regarded as the Great Divide between Relative Youth and Post-Youth. Sure enough, the day after my birthday (all right, so I was one day past forty already, but it was my *birthday*), I showed up, as good as my word, at the rec center indoor pool.

There were drawbacks to my exercise of choice, the most serious being that I didn't know how to swim. For the first year, I lay on my back, watched the blue squares on the ceiling, and flutter-kicked my way across the pool. Twenty minutes of that, four times a week for a year, and I was able to add a backstroke to my repertoire. I had always been almost able to do a crooked sidestroke—on my left side only, for ten yards at most—so I worked on that, too, laboring a length or two each morning like a salmon heading upstream before I flipped over on my back to finish my laps. Eventually, remembering how my kids' swim instructors cried, "Elbow up out of the water!" with each stroke, I parleyed my pathetic sidestroke into a bona fide Australian crawl that now takes me back and forth at my leisure through a half-hour swim every day. (How many laps? Don't know. I have other things to think about.)

The main reward of my after-forty exercise program hasn't been learning to swim or staying in shape, more or less, but the company I keep. You meet a lot of interesting people in the Iowa City rec center locker room, women of all ages, with first names only and nothing to hide. I spent about two years looking forward to my morning chats with Ellen, for example, before I learned her last name from another locker room friend, who told me the bad news that Ellen—who was a little older than my mother—had fallen and broken her hip. I went to see her at the hospital, pledged rides to the pool when she was ready for them, and a few months later, as a result of a broken hip, our friendship took a leap forward. Today, Ellen and I are half of a very select group of veteran swimmers with a standing date for breakfast at the Hamburg Inn after our Saturday swim.

If you were at another table, you would see us sitting here in our favorite booth (the only one with the comfy cushioned seat). You would make a point of looking our way, although, like the rest of the customers, you'd be discreet about it, offering a smile and nod if any of us caught you watching. We are a group to see: Sarah, who puts salt on her oatmeal—excuse me, on her *porridge*—and even raises her eyebrows with a Yorkshire accent; Ellen with her metal cane and her hearty laugh, holding my arm on the way to our table (how deceptively frail she must look to the rest of the world!); our forthright friend Mori, whose lipstick is as miraculously red after she swims as it was before; and me, my long hair damp and my bangs stick straight. No wonder people steal a look.

Not the wait staff, though. They never look at anyone funny at the Burg. Our favorites, like the curly-haired young man with the killer smile and four little rings in one ear, or the black-haired young woman who likes to wear her headscarf tied in the back, peasant style—they are hearty and friendly; they laugh with us. They say, "Oatmeal all around?" They say, "Nuts and raisins?" We say, "And brown sugar." Except for Sarah, who says, "Hold the sugar, if you please." In Yorkshire, they don't put sugar on their oatmeal, and they don't call it oatmeal either, which is why we are The Porridge Club: Sarah, Ellen, Mori, and I, and Brenda, our long-distance member who left us for the tenure track in Champaign-Urbana.

Some of us even have an official T-shirt. On the front, it's the usual: "Hamburg Inn No. 2, Iowa City, Iowa." On the back, in iron-on letters, we added "The Porridge Club" and our motto: "First we swim. Then we eat." Ellen wore hers one Saturday, with a turtleneck underneath it to keep her arms warm and her terrycloth turban to complete the look. We kept making her turn around to show people: "First we swim. Then we eat." Watching us from another table, who would ever guess that we were going to live forever?

IN IT FOR THE LONG HAUL

A Bicycle Meant for Me

JUNE 2013

W hen I was a kid, I always got my sister's hand-me-downs. She's four years older, so when she got a brand-new blue-and-silver twenty-six-inch Schwinn three-speed with hand brakes, I inherited her old twenty-incher with its fat tires, green fenders, foot brakes, and only the one unchangeable gear to pedal in, effectively making it a no-speed. The twenty-incher was probably the cooler bike, at least by today's standards, but I didn't know that then.

In my Milwaukee neighborhood, bicycles were not really a mode of transportation — though we did ride occasionally to the McDonald's in Cudahy — nor, heaven forbid, a fitness program. They were a thing you did for fun: "Wanna ride bikes?" Depending on what TV show or mystery book had most recently captured our imagination, our bikes might be helicopters (from a program called *Whirlybirds*, we were copter pilots named Chuck and P. T.) or horses, or little blue coupes (Nancy Drew), or popcorn machines, where you turned the bike upside down and used the pedals like cranks to make handfuls of grass or apple blossoms fly out from between the wheel and the fender. That worked better with a tricycle actually.

My little brother — who, incidentally, couldn't be expected to ride a hand-me-down *girl's* bike, could he? — was a bicycle accident magnet. At age seven or eight, he broke his two front teeth off when he went down face first over the handlebars in the alley behind our house. Five or six years later, he took a corner too fast and broke both arms the night before he was to compete in his first junior golf tournament.

Apart from getting my foot caught in the rear wheel spokes as a passenger on the back fender of my cousin Monda's bike, I saved my share of childhood stitches and broken bones for tightrope walking on the back porch rail and the deliberate misuse of folding lawn furniture.

Flash forward to the first Christmas after John and I were married. This was back in the Seventies—the 1970s, I should perhaps specify. We were both still in college. He had a semester to go, and I had my whole senior year left. (Wait a minute, wait a minute, our kids used to say. How come *you* can get *married* when you're still in school? The answer is obvious: John and I were exceptionally mature for our age.) That first year, we lived in a one-bedroom apartment upstairs from Aunt Madeline, who was born in the old country and gave us a huge break on the rent in return for shoveling snow and cutting the grass in her double lot. She made us use a nonmotorized lawn mower, the kind that makes a lovely clickety-tick-tick-tick-tick when you push it. She had an electric lawn mower, but she was afraid we'd run over the cord. Aunt Madeline never understood how exceptionally mature we were for our age.

So there it was, our first Christmas morning as husband and wife, and I'm waiting with my eyes closed so I won't see what John is bringing up the front hall stairs into the living room, where we've set up our very first Christmas tree, decorated with paint-them-yourself wooden cut-out ornaments and low-cost candy canes. When I heard a clickety-tick-tick-tick noise, you can be sure that it was very hard not to take a peek, but John said, "Wait! Wait! Wait!" and went back downstairs for more.

It better not be a lawn mower, I was thinking.

When I opened my eyes, I couldn't believe what I saw: not one but two brand new green-and-silver twenty-six-inch *five*-speeds—a matching pair—one girl's, one boy's.

I knew in that moment that our marriage would last a lifetime.

That bike was the best surprise present I had ever received. It was like the ending of a Flannery O'Connor story (but without the dead bodies): "totally unexpected" and "totally right."

In retrospect, it seems as if we rode those bikes everywhere together—once the snow melted—for years and years. In reality, the birth of our son two and a half years later curtailed our matching bike trips pretty effectively. As a matter of fact, the last year I applied for a bicycle license plate, as required in West Allis, Wisconsin, was 1975, the year that Jeff was born.

Dusty though they were, our matching bikes came with us from Wisconsin to Iowa, where, sad to say, John's soon disappeared. He said I should say that he lent it to a saxophone player, along with a ten-dollar bill, and he hasn't seen either one since. He also said I should say that if the aforementioned saxophone player is reading this and still has the bike, we'd love to get it back. (You can keep the ten dollars.)

In Iowa City, the bicycle became our major mode of transportation. John scrounged up a recycled bike for work, and I rode my formerly matching one to campus on Tuesday afternoons. (Not to brag, but coming home was all uphill.) A few years later, I rode my bike to work in the publication department at ACT—American College Testing—where so many Iowa Writers' Workshop grads have found day jobs to support their writing habit. And I still recall, with a pang of parental nostalgia, the first time our son Jeff rode downtown on his bike—a twenty-incher not too different from the one I inherited from my sister. Each of our three children has fallen off a bike at one time or another. Stitches were sometimes required, but nobody knocked any teeth out. It was their father who learned the hard way that you can't zip up your jacket while coasting around a corner—*Look, Ma, no hands!*—at the bottom of a hill.

John has a different old bike now, inherited from our friend Leslee Becker when she left Iowa City in the late 1980s. He rode it to work year-round for more than thirty years, weather permitting or not. I'm afraid he still enjoys coasting down the long sidewalk on Dubuque Street during Iowa City's modest rush hour, his hands behind his head, occasionally calling to the drivers in the cars that inch toward downtown beside him, "My transportation costs are zero!"

I have a photo of John and his bike ankle-deep in the water-covered street in front of our house. It was early in the Great Flood of 2008, and we had taken a ride out to the Coralville Reservoir on the last day that it was possible to do so. If I were in the photo, you could see that I was still riding my Christmas bike with a red West Allis license plate that expired in 1976.

Author's Note: My sister, the one who always got a new bike, claims that it wasn't my foot but hers that got stuck in the rear wheel spokes while she was riding on the back fender of our cousin Monda's bike. If my sister is right, then she was the one who got swooped up in Uncle Joe's arms and carried around the corner to the house, where her tears were dried and her shoe and sock were carefully removed, her foot gently flexed and examined and soaked in warm water and Epsom salts while she ate any number of cookies. If she's right—and her recall of detail suggests that she is—then all I can say is, whose rear-wheel spokes did *my* foot get stuck in? Also, I didn't get any cookies.

NIGHT SWIMMING

When the First Shall Be Last, or Vice Versa

SEPTEMBER 2002

B y the time you read this, summer will be over—not according to the calendar, perhaps, but we all know that
calling September 22 the first day of fall is nothing but
wishful thinking. In Iowa City, summer ends when they close
City Park Pool on Labor Day at eight o'clock in the evening,
surely one of the saddest hours of the year.

It used to be nine o'clock. I can recall specific last-nights-in-
the-pool from the years when it stayed open long enough to need
the ballpark style lights overhead and the shining globes in the
sides of the pool that light the water from below. Minutes before
nine o'clock, you'd stop and turn around at the locker room door
to take it all in one last time—the humid air turning the overhead lights into clusters of stars on a stick, the whole pool transformed into a trembling blue crystal. You'd stand there, dripping,
until you'd seen enough to tide you over until next season.

One time late in August, I was swimming leisurely laps just
before closing, when a full moon appeared, huge and haloed
and framed by oak trees—such good timing! The next night,
I brought my friend Sarah to see it, but nine o'clock came and
went, and the moon failed to show. Sarah didn't seem to mind
that I had promised the moon but couldn't deliver. She and I
leaned on our cars in the dark and talked until the park closed
at ten.

My family and I have been swimming at City Park long
enough to remember the old roofless wooden building where you
could look up through the crown of an oak tree while you took

your shower. We were sad to see the building go. For a long time we missed the numbered baskets full of T-shirts and sandals, the wooden bathroom stalls that closed with a hook-and-eye, the sun that used to dry and disinfect the concrete floor instead incubating it by beating down on the roof. The new building is nice enough, I guess, with its colorfully painted concrete blocks, stainless steel stalls (at least two of which have doors that stay closed), and a roof to protect against the elements, vandals, and the threat to modesty posed by low-flying hot-air balloons.

In the late 1980s, when the children were at that in-between age—old enough to go off the diving boards and young enough to want me there to applaud when they did—Jeff, Liz, Lauren, and my husband John used to shuffle to the back of the line until all four of them were up at once, two on the high boards and two on the low.

I didn't go off any board in those days, and I still don't do the high dive, although I did it once, during those in-between years, after a kid I didn't even know happened to notice me waiting in line, only to chicken out (as usual) when I got to the ladder. We went to the pool almost every night, and that kid was always there goading me, pointing his finger and clucking. I told him to show a little respect; I was old enough to be his mother. He said, "So? You're still chicken."

By the end of July, I'd had it. Eyes closed and heart pounding, I jumped off the high dive. The rest of the flying Stefaniaks applauded. "Isn't it a great feeling?" my daughter asked me as I hauled myself out of the water. "I'll never do it again," I said. But at least I could confront my tormentor. I found the little creep climbing out of the diving well himself (the low-board side, I might add).

"Hey," I said, looking down at him from the full height of my accomplishment. "I went off the high dive."

He shrugged skinny shoulders. "So?"

"What do you mean, 'so'?"

"I didn't see you do it."

In more recent years, my husband and I have sharpened our competitive edges on more substantive achievements. I can put on my swim cap and goggles while treading water in the deep end, for example. John can swim underwater for the whole length of a lap lane. For several years running, including this one, my husband has been the First Citizen in the Pool on opening day, Memorial Day weekend. (Some ducks paddling in the icy water challenged John's claim to the title one year, until someone remembered that ducks don't pay taxes.)

But the most impressive of my husband's aquatic achievements has to be—well, let me give you a firsthand account. John filed this report last year.

"As you probably already heard—it was on NPR and CNN—the Golden Trophy for the Last Citizen Out of the Pool Contest is once again in my possession. The sound bite on NPR had the mayor thanking me on behalf of the city for providing such an inspiring example of Good Citizenship.

"My competitors this year were in league with each other and crafty, but, alas, ill-informed. With only minutes to go, they—five wily sixth graders—attempted to distract me by yapping among themselves (at a volume intended to include me and any deaf pensioners within one mile) that two of their number were going to be the Last to Leap Off the High Dive Holding Hands, that another was poised to become Last One to Touch the Bottom, yet another the Last to Swim Backward Under the Ropes, etc., all the while apparently unaware that only One Feat really mattered, that only One Champion would be named: Last Citizen Out of the Pool.

"And in the end, it was I who triumphed! Exhibiting rare solidarity, the City Council members in attendance ganged up on the poor sky-writer pilot, who eventually agreed to go back up and respell my name correctly."

John's triumph this year is history by now, I'm sure, although there was one Labor Day—a chilly, overcast one—when my husband failed to snag the Golden Trophy. He seemed well on his way to an easy victory that year, with only one shivering kid left in the water as the hour approached. The little boy's mother was waiting with a towel at the pool's edge, no doubt trying to coax him out, while John paddled slowly, slowly across the deep end toward the ladder. The clock was running out. The kid was turning blue. The trophy was almost in the bag when John heard the mother say, "It won't be much longer now, Jeffrey! There's only one guy left in the pool."

OUTSIDE THE COMFORT ZONE

WHAT DID I SAY?

Fear and Babbling in the Speaker's Corner

APRIL 2001

Perhaps you've been there. You have a meeting scheduled or a class underway—and the boss walks in unannounced, or the principal, looking stern. Or maybe you thought you were going to facilitate a little discussion with five or six colleagues, but the whole room starts filling up. Everyone looks at you expectantly. You start to sweat. Then you babble. The audience understands from your rapid-fire speech and too-bright tone that you have prepared a presentation and intend to deliver it, come hell or high water.

Trouble is, the audience is only half right. You have prepared no presentation, unless two or three points on a sticky note constitute a presentation. Your only objective at this point is to build, between you and them, a wall of words that will deflect all questions and comments, challenging or otherwise. Two or three minutes into your babbling, the Scheherazade effect kicks in: if you stop talking now, you know you are dead.

No matter how long you've been teaching or giving speeches, a bout of sweat-and-babble can strike. Last week, I volunteered to lead a discussion with our graduate students on a pedagogical issue of interest to all. I was expecting eight students to attend. I was not expecting the director of the Center for Henry James Studies, the director of the World Literature Program, and the director of Composition to show up. They were simply fellow teachers, interested in the topic, which was, ironically, how to improve small group discussion, but their unexpected presence set me first to sweating and then to babbling. Anyone planning to make a comment or ask a question would have to storm my wall of words. A few brave souls tried to speak, but they didn't get far. I seized every comment and used it to launch another torrent of talk. When it was all over, I had very little idea of what I had said. Many sweat-and-babble experiences are followed by a state of merciful amnesia.

Sometimes sweating and babbling, like stream of consciousness or automatic writing, produces something that makes some kind of sense. When I was interviewing for my job as a college professor, the grueling day-long process culminated with a presentation to the English department faculty on a designated topic. A note I wrote to a friend at the time tells me that I spoke about the author/narrator as a fictional creation, taking my cue from a Borges story called "Borges and I," which ends with the line "I do not know which one of us has written this page." If I had not come across that note to my friend recently, I could not tell you what my presentation was about. I might not even know which one of us had given the talk. My memory of the speech, like my mind at the time, is completely blank.

I hasten to add, in case the department chair ever happens to read this, that I prepared exhaustively for that presentation. The problem that time was the condition of my notes. I am an inveterate rewriter and second-guesser, frequently afflicted by last-minute inspiration. My notes had started out neatly typed, but by late afternoon, every page was crammed with arrows, cross-outs, and scrawled additions. I think I could have made them out anyway, had I been standing at a podium with the pages spread before me. Unfortunately, I had to do the talk while sitting at the head of a long table in the Rare Book Room, with professors to my immediate left and right. I couldn't put those messy notes right under their noses on the table, so I left them in my lap. Then I pulled my chair up to the table in such a way that they were invisible to my neighbors—and to me.

I was already sweating, so for the next thirty minutes, I gripped the handout I'd distributed, and I babbled. A few days later, they told me I had the job. Many faculty members complimented me on my presentation. I only wish I could remember what I said.

The most terrifying sweat-and-babble occasion I have survived so far was an acceptance speech I had to make at the annual meeting of the Wisconsin Library Association.

Except for the speech, the occasion was a happy one. The Library Association had chosen a collection of my short stories as the best book written by a Wisconsin author that year. They flew me from Omaha to the Grand Geneva Resort (formerly the Playboy Club) on lovely Lake Geneva, about forty miles from my hometown of Milwaukee. There they treated me in the manner of an award-winning author—readings, book signings, wining and dining—a manner to which I decided I could easily become accustomed. The climax of the two-day conference was the awards dinner, a sit-down affair in the ballroom. Imagine my surprise when the chairwoman of the Literary Awards Committee leaned over the dessert we'd just been served to tell me that she and I would go up to the stage together a few minutes from now, she would introduce me, and then I would give my acceptance speech.

Only a mouthful of cheesecake preventing me from croaking, "Acceptance speech?"

For the next half hour, I watched the Librarian of the Year, various champion fundraisers, and other awardees go up on stage to accept their saucer-sized bronze medallions, after which they stepped up to the microphone and delivered their heartfelt thanks in witty speeches of five minutes or less. I was concentrating on keeping my dinner down when the chairwoman of the Literary Awards Committee stood up and whispered, "Let's go!"

We threaded our way through a minefield of round tables to

the front. Onstage I looked out at some two hundred librarians and guests, many of them still enjoying their cheesecake. The chairwoman introduced me and said nice things about my book, even quoting a favorite passage. Then she stepped graciously aside and the microphone was mine.

All the people at all the tables looked at me with shining faces.

I don't know what I said, but I got a couple of laughs before I was finished, and no one at the Literary Awards Committee table turned gray or looked sick while I spoke. When I stopped babbling, the librarians applauded—a good sign, I hoped. Clutching my medallion to my chest, I followed the chairwoman back to our table, encouraged by nods and smiles from well-wishers as we passed by. I waited until the final speech was underway before whispering to the chairwoman, "How was it?"

She patted my hand—a gesture of sympathy? or congratulation? I'll never know—and said, after the tiniest of pauses, "Great."

Whenever I feel bad about things I've bungled in this way, I remind myself that even the President and Vice President of the United States go blank from time to time. I figure the sweat-and-babble syndrome is responsible for many of the malapropisms, misquotations, and unfortunate remarks we hear every day from politicians and other public figures. They know what a terrible thing it is to lose one's mind—especially in the middle of a speaking engagement.

WHERE THE GIRLS (AND BOYS) ARE

Just Call Me Coach

SEPTEMBER 1999

What with all the hoopla about the US women's soccer team winning the World Cup last summer, I feel it's time to reveal a little secret from my past.

I was a female soccer coach.

For one brief shining season in 1989 and two less shining seasons that followed, I was head coach of an Iowa City Kickers team from Horn Elementary School. Eleven- and twelve-year-olds. Girls and boys.

I think I was the only female head coach in Kickers that year. I may have been the only head coach in Kickers history—maybe the only head coach in the history of organized sports—who had never in my life participated at any level on any organized team of any kind, unless you count a once-a-month couples bowling league back in Milwaukee. (In the women's column on the ratings sheet, I was always dead last.)

I tried to impress the depth of my inexperience on the Kickers commissioner who called me that night in January, having noted on my daughter's registration form that her mother would be willing to "help out." I'd imagined giving rides or providing snacks, maybe typing up the telephone tree. The commissioner had something else in mind.

"I can't coach the team!" I told him. "I don't know anything about soccer." I'd never even seen a Kickers game. Except for my son Jeff's one-season foray into Little League (thank God no one asked us to coach *that*), I had so far escaped the whole kid's athletics routine. I considered myself lucky. The soccer commissioner made it clear that my luck had run out.

"If you don't coach, there won't be any team," he said grimly.

"How can that be?" My daughter was the only new kid. "Who coached before?"

The young man who had coached the children from first grade through fourth had gone off to college in September, he said.

"Who coached them last fall?" I asked.

There was a little silence. Then the commissioner said, "A parent." Pressed for details, he revealed that the parent in question was a South American who had probably started playing soccer when he was two.

"So what happened to him?"

There was a longer silence. I never did find out exactly why the guy quit, but I gathered that he knew a little too much about soccer. That, at least, was something of which no one could accuse me. I knew nothing.

The commissioner assured me that my job as head coach would be mainly administrative. All I had to do was pick up the team's supply of balls and cones (Cones? I was thinking), show up at the games on Sunday afternoon, and maybe get some parents to help me run practice twice a week.

"Practice?" I asked.

"No big deal," the commissioner said. "A few drills, maybe a scrimmage."

Drills? Scrimmage?

My ignorance was vast. At our first practice, the boy I'd recruited to haul the big string bag of balls and cones out of the car happened to spot the stack of library books I'd pored over the night before, trying to come up with a soccer practice plan.

He groaned. "We're not going to read *books*, are we?"

"Not to worry, Matt," I said. "I'll do all the reading around here."

I still don't know how I got away with it. The bravest thing I have ever done was to go to my first game, clutching my player chart (that showed me who went where on the field) and realizing on the way to the park that I didn't know where the coach was supposed to stand. My husband, who'd done his part for gender equity as a Bluebird mother when our daughter Liz was seven, abdicated all responsibility for my coaching endeavors. You could tell he didn't even want to come to the games. I think he was afraid for me. Or maybe he was afraid somebody would ask him to coach too. Or instead.

We won that first game, by the way.

So there were compensations, the most important being the Return of the Girls. The Horn-E team had followed the usual pattern, gender balanced in the early grades, more and more girls dropping out as they got older, until the twelve-member team I inherited was down to only two girls, not counting my daughter. When word got out, though, that the new coach was somebody's mom, three girls who'd dropped out returned to the team and two more girls (new to the game but outstanding athletes both) joined us. We ended up with eight girls—at least twice the number on any of the sixth-grade teams we played—including three future All-State runners and a tennis champ. Among the boys were wrestlers-to-be and state champion football players, one of them a future University of Iowa Hawkeye.

I came up with one truly brilliant coaching strategy during my career: the Saturday morning practice.

Our midweek practices were squirrely at best. After being cooped up in school all day, eleven- and twelve-year-olds are not interested in waiting in line to kick the ball around the cones. But at 7:30 on Saturday morning, still half asleep, they are much more malleable creatures. At that hour, Willow Creek Park was empty except for us. Kids showed up one by one. They got a ball, started warming up. Our wonderful assistant coach Joe Buckwalter strolled over from home, coffee cup in hand, his position as team physician for the Iowa Hawkeyes adding some luster to the entire coaching staff. One or two younger siblings might show up to watch or chase balls, often joined by somebody's dog. Spring practice started in March, so the balls we dribbled and passed cut through frost on the grass. One time a light snow fell. I remember that practice like a silent movie: the white field, the green paths of the balls, the children running with clouds of steamy breath over their heads.

I remember other moments too. Like the time the game was so close that Justin offered me fifteen dollars if I would just put him back in please, "Coach, please Coach, *please.*" Or the time that Kyla wouldn't let me wipe the blood off her pretty face after she'd recovered from an elbow to the nose, because she wanted to go back in looking fierce.

All those kids called me Coach.

As for the final record, if memory serves me, we were undefeated that first season, split our second season (three and three), and it was downhill from there. Our skills were great, but I'm afraid the few plays I tried to map out just didn't go over very well. The team suspected (correctly) that I'd gotten them out of a book. Even so, with apologies to my fellow former head coach, the late Vince Lombardi, winning is *not* the only thing. Ask any one of those kids. We learned a lot about each other. We had a good time.

SCUBA

Do? (or Don't)

Standing at the edge of the pool with my weight belt digging into my hipbones, and my air tank hanging heavy on the back of my inflatable vest, and my feet transformed into foot-and-a-half-long fins, and my face half hidden by a plastic mask from which a snorkel sticks up like a pink periscope, and my teeth and lips keeping a life-and-death grip on the regulator (a thing like an oversized pacifier that you put in your mouth and breathe from), I have to ask myself this question: Who came up with the brilliant idea of recreational diving?

I figure one (or both) of two groups is probably to blame. Either manufacturers of scuba equipment were looking for a way to expand their market, or a bunch of sunburned beachcombing scuba divers were looking for a way to support their habit. Somehow, those enterprising beachcombers became the Professional Association of Diving Instructors (PADI). Technical writers, graphic designers, and educational consultants were hired to produce a jazzy line of instructional materials. Colorful brochures and humorous videos went out into the world, encouraging those who "live life on the edge" to "GO DIVE." Before long, dive shops were selling air tanks and wet suits in places like Omaha, Nebraska (where we have five dive shops to choose from). A new recreational industry was born.

But how did I get involved? It wasn't the blurbs on the back of the GO DIVE brochure that drew me in. I do not "live life on the edge," nor do I "find pleasure in a pure adrenaline high." On the other hand, "exploring the secrets of a sunken wreck" and "experiencing close encounters with fascinating species in exotic corners of the globe" sounded pretty good—especially the exotic corners of the globe part. (The species maybe I could do without.)

Mostly though, it was my daughter Lauren. At Cornell University she discovered that she could get her freshman and sophomore physical education requirements out of the way in just two all-day weekends per year if she took scuba diving. The fact that scuba would come in handy for a marine biologist (her major) was frosting on the no-gym-class cake.

"You'll love it, Mom!" she said. "You can be my diving buddy!" (One always dives with a buddy.)

What mother could resist an invitation like that? Throw in our upcoming, once-in-a-lifetime family Christmas trip to Key Largo—diving and snorkeling capital of the US—and I think you can see why I signed up.

My mother couldn't, though. When she heard that I was taking scuba diving at Creighton, she said, "Oh, Mary Helen, you're not. What on earth for? You're not going in the ocean, are you?"

I mentioned Key Largo.

"There are sharks in the ocean," she said. "They're attacking people."

I didn't tell my mother, but at this point sharks are the least of my worries. Scuba diving is more hazardous, and infinitely more complicated, than I thought. You have to worry about atmospheres and equalization and the dangers of lung overexpansion—which is quite a separate thing from the trouble Lloyd Bridges was always having on *Sea Hunt* with "the bends." You have to remember how to assemble your equipment and never to hold your breath. You have to remember which knob to turn and which rings to pull and which button does what.

When you make a mistake, you pay.

One minute I was sitting on the bottom of the pool with the rest of the class, feeling only slightly claustrophobic, all suited up and breathing, ten feet under in the diving well. We were watching the instructor's hand signals: to go up (thumb up), we were to let all the air out of our inflatable vests (a.k.a. our Buoyancy Control Devices, or BCDs) by pushing this little button with our thumb. He held up the thing with the button to demonstrate. Then we slowly, slowly kick our way like this—he let his fingers do the kicking—to the surface. His silent lecture completed, he gave us the okay sign: Did we get it? Were we ready? We signed it back at him: Okay. The next thing I knew, I had shot up to the surface and popped into the air.

I pushed the wrong button.

Instead of deflating my vest I'd filled it like a balloon, and the balloon had risen to the surface like a bubble in a soda bottle— a very apt analogy since, if I'd shot to the surface from deeper waters, then my lungs might have burst like a bubble too.

My instructor's head was the first to surface after mine; the others were slowly, slowly kicking their way up. "Well, Mary," he said as soon as he'd taken the regulator out of his mouth, "I hate to tell you this, but you're dead."

In class, nobody wants to be my buddy.

Once, when the instructor was trying to show me something at the surface, I sprayed him in the face with a blast of water by placing my regulator in the pool, business side up. (Always put your regulator in the water mouthpiece down.) Another time I hit him in the side of the head with my snorkel.

I like to blame these things on being left-handed in a right-handed world, but maybe I'm just a klutz.

Maybe that's what draws me to the water; for a klutz, it can be a more forgiving medium than air. It thwarts gravity and confers grace. I like that. Besides, I grew up on *Sea Hunt*. Every Sunday afternoon, Lloyd Bridges narrated tales of underwater adventure while divers swam gracefully across the black-and-white television screen, his voice accompanied by the bubbling streams of their underwater breathing, their fins scissoring through the depths. Once you're in the water—if you can get your ears equalized

and your vest properly inflated to achieve neutral buoyancy—
you forget the cumbersome equipment. You're weightless and free.
Who knows? A couple of months from now, after swimming silently with my daughter through underwater forests, after skim-
ming over coral reefs unearthly in their shapes and colors, I may
be signing up for Scuba II.

If I don't get eaten by a shark.

TRUE PERILS
OF PARENTING

THE END OF THE WORLD AS WE KNOW IT

Little Girl Lost

APRIL 1998

Early in March, I drove my daughter Liz back to school in St. Louis. After four spring-break days of laughing and talking at the kitchen table, groaning together in fitting rooms, aqua-jogging at the rec center pool, and heading out to Hofer's Danceland—with Liz, her sister Lauren, two admirably coordinated friends of theirs, and my good sport of a husband—for Sunday night ballroom dancing, all that was left to me now was a goodbye hug and the long drive back to Iowa City. My middle child was gone again, her bed empty, the bathroom desolately available until May.

If I had known that life with children was fraught with such tragedy, I might have had second thoughts about having three of them.

Oh, I know much worse things could have happened than watching them grow up. There was a time, in fact, when Liz was small, when I felt certain that something terrible would happen to her. She was a lanky, blue-eyed child with a mane of wild blond hair, her arms and long legs covered by a fine layer of golden down. No child so illuminated could possibly endure in the dark world, I thought. I used to hold my breath when she pedaled off down the sidewalk on her way around the block, wobbly and tall on the seat of a hand-me-down bicycle, hair flying, knees and elbows out at sharp angles. In an agony of suspense, I waited for her to reappear at the other end of the block, trying not to watch the corner she would turn so sharply that laws of physics would have to be defied to keep her from teetering over into a damaged heap on the pavement, longing to hear her husky "Yo!" or "Whew!" as she braked to a halt at the foot of our stairs. She used to hate her voice. "I sound like a boy," she complained. (I must have sounded the same husky way when I was small; our voices are so nearly identical now that we fool people on the phone without even trying.) She hated the down on her legs, too. Having survived to adolescence in spite of my forebodings, she shaved it all off.

You'd think that I'd be used to it by now. I've been through it all before. Four years ago, when we took Jeff, our firstborn, off to Madison, we pulled the old station wagon crammed with stuff into the unloading zone in front of his dorm and heard R.E.M. blasting from another freshman's open window. I recognized the song: "It's the End of the World as We Know It (and I Feel Fine)." No kidding, I thought about the end of the world part. I did not feel fine.

It starts so much sooner, though, their long, slow departure from the center of your life. Often, there's a bicycle involved. The earliest twinges I felt at my son's independence came one day in summer when he was ten, the first time I let him ride downtown to play video games at the mall with his friends. I stood outside—at the bottom of the same front steps where I waited for Liz to come around the block—and watched Jeff ride away. This was in Iowa City, and we lived only a few blocks from downtown, for heaven's sake, but it was still a big step, the first time I'd let him go anywhere all by himself. Maybe he was only nine. Is that possible? I don't remember. I do remember the back of his neck as he pedaled away from me, taking my breath away with him.

The bicycles are only a prelude to the most traumatic event in childrearing: the first time they drive off in a car. All you can do is watch, left behind, helpless to protect them from road rage, brake failure, inattentive drivers, and the dangers of holding a Coke in one hand and changing the radio station with the other, while steering with their knees.

Friends made a video once of our three children and theirs gently examining sea creatures taken from tanks in my husband's office in the biology building on campus. Their sleeves rolled up, the children are plunging their arms into the glass tank of their choice and coming up with a dripping starfish or a purple sea urchin, or maybe a gristly glob of sea squirt, aimed at the camera. There is a sequence of Liz, at about age six, the wild mane of hair tumbling around her shoulders. She's looking up at the camera with her usual please-love-me smile (no braces yet, only perfect baby teeth), answering questions in her six-year-old voice about the starfish she's holding up in both hands, like an offering, for the edification of the viewer.

The first time I saw that video, years after it was made, it almost knocked me flat, so overcome was I with grief at having lost those three beautiful children on the screen: not only Liz but three-year-old Lauren—too small and shy to do anything but duck her head and hold up a Barbie doll when the camera approached—and Jeff at age nine with his delicate neck and little boy voice. They were all lost to me forever, turned by time into handsome teenagers, I realized as I watched. Even now, when Lauren's a high school junior with one year to go and counting and I have to call Jeff or Liz long-distance, I still can't get over the fact—if I'm so foolish as to stop and think about it—that I'll never see the little girl with the husky voice again, no matter how often I play the video to hear her say, after a quick toss of her head to fling her hair back, "Now this, you see, is a starfish. I don't know if it's a boy or a girl. With starfish, it's hard to tell. But this part here is the mouth, see? I'll hold it up closer. Can you see?"

MOTHER AND CHILD REUNION

What I Did on My Summer Vacation

I drove 3,969 miles — with my mother.

In less than two weeks, I drove from Iowa City to Milwaukee (where my mother lives) to Macon, Georgia (where my mother is from) to South Florida (where my son now lives) to St. Louis (middle daughter) and back. My mother, whose maximum highway driving speed is forty to fifty miles per hour, never took the wheel. She did her share of the driving from the passenger seat.

I thought that my mother and I had resolved our mother-daughter issues, that our relationship had reached a plateau of mutual respect and affection. Either I was wrong, or there is no plateau that won't crumble under the pressure of 3,969 miles in a car together. One day into the trip, I understood exactly why my sister — who spent part of her summer vacation on a Mediterranean cruise — had given my mother a string of worry beads from Greece and wished us good luck, instead of going with us.

We hadn't even cleared Illinois before we started arguing, amazed at the heat we brought to topics like whether the left lane really is for passing. The books on tape I'd brought were no help. They always seemed to reach a point where the frequency of cursing exceeded my mother's tolerance level. Having already fast-forwarded through the sexy parts, by the time we cut out the expletives, we'd have lost the thread of the plot.

Stopping for the night caused more trouble. I had forgotten that my mother needs a light on to fall asleep. To stay asleep, I need darkness. Every night, I woke up three or four times, thinking it was morning. To a woman like my mother, accustomed to rising at 4:00 or 4:30 a.m., anybody who wants to sleep past daylight looks like a slacker anyway. At quarter to six one morning, I heard her mutter as she got up, "Well, I can't stay in bed all day."

Lack of sleep takes its toll on a person. Halfway through Tennessee, I found myself thinking that if my mother clutched one more time at the medals she wears around her neck, I might have to reach over and strangle her with them. On the other hand, who could blame her? We saw more accidents in two weeks than I'd seen in all the rest of my life put together. My mother had countless opportunities — some of them justified — to utter her four favorite words: "Watch out, Mary Helen!"

Mom's holy medals aside, it was nothing short of a miracle that we didn't get into an accident ourselves, especially in the harrowing moment when my right rear tire blew out — not, thank God, on I-75 but on the curve of a shoulderless two-lane road between Haddock, Georgia, and Milledgeville. Seems we'd picked up a screwdriver-sized spike, possibly during our visit to Aunt Molly's salvage yard. Luckily, my mother and two of her sisters were in the car when the tire blew. ("What was that?" "Oh my Lord!" "Watch out, Mary Helen!") Without their support and advice, I would have had to handle the situation myself, aided only by a very nice Baldwin County law officer who saw our Volvo limp off the road. A soft-spoken fellow, gray at the temples, in a crisp white shirt and tie, the officer radioed Bud's Wrecking in Haddock and waited with us for the truck to arrive. Aunt Shirley asked him if he was married.

In Georgia, aunts and great-aunts kept saying how nice it was that my mother and I had made this trip together. Guiltily, I sipped sweet tea.

In Florida, my mother and I put up such a good front that my son didn't even know we were crabby. Jeff was eager to show us things. We saw his new car, his new apartment (with the lovely pool), his new clothes, his new furniture. (The family picture I'd sent him was framed on his dresser.) He showed us where he worked—a video production outfit. He was tanned and handsome, wearing a bright green checked shirt he never would have worn in Iowa City. "That shirt looks nice on you," I told him. I could see he was pleased to hear it.

Mom and I maintained our uneasy truce. When I went for an early morning swim at Jeff's place, she came down to the pool with me to make sure I wouldn't drown.

"Oh, Mom," I said.

She reminded me of the time I nearly drowned in a motel pool on the way to Georgia years ago. I reminded her that I couldn't swim (back then) because she wouldn't let me take lessons. To change the subject, she said, "Do you do this for exercise or fun?"

"Exercise," I told her, as I threw my arm over my head in a leisurely backstroke.

She looked doubtful but strolled around the pool while I swam back and forth. I showed her what I could do: backstroke, side stroke, breaststroke (sort of), and the crawl, with my face in the water and everything. *Look at me, Mom!* I was thinking.

At the beach in Ft. Lauderdale, Mom explored the shops across the street—swimwear, souvenirs—while Jeff and I waded in the clearest, warmest water imaginable, waves breaking around our ankles. I regretted leaving my wet swimsuit at the apartment and, in a moment of reckless inspiration, decided to go across the street and buy another one. I expected an argument from my mother, but all she said was, "Hurry up, whatever you do. It's hot." She and Jeff sat at a sidewalk café with a cool drink while I sweated it out in the fitting room.

Buying that swimsuit was one of the best ideas I've ever had. Jeff and I made a heap of our clothes on the beach, shoes on top to keep them from blowing away, and spent the next twenty minutes throwing ourselves into the waves like a couple of little kids.

Jeff might have been ten years old instead of twenty-four. For that matter, I might have been ten myself.

And my mother? She watched us from under the palm trees that bordered the beach. When we joined her there in the shade, dripping, and carrying our sandy clothes, she said, "It's much cooler on this side of the street." And then, "That suit looks nice on you, Mary Helen."

I was pleased to hear it. I hope she could tell.

SITTING IN THE LONELY SEAT
ON THE LONG WAY HOME

O ur youngest daughter, the one who has been speaking poetry all her life, has gone off to college.

Not so many weeks ago, we left her on the granite steps of Baker Hall at Cornell University in Ithaca, New York, a thousand miles from where I sit and write these words. She was on her way to take a placement test at the time, worried about being late for it and about all the French she'd forgotten, distracted from goodbyes. "Tu vas souvenir beaucoup," I told her— *You'll remember plenty*—and tried to make her hug me again, claiming that she hadn't yet. Assez! she must have been thinking. *Enough!* One more peck on the cheek—and she was libre at last.

Lauren has always had her way with words. This is the daughter who, at age three, climbed up on the kitchen counter to look at the thermometer hanging outside the window and announced, "Yep, it's a quarter to Easter." When we finally acquired a kitten the children had long lobbied for, it was Lauren, then six, who sighed, "At last, in our house, a mammal that walks on four legs." (Five two-legged ones were already on the premises, you see.) I once overheard her explaining the sex life of crickets to a fellow preschooler this way: "First the boys sing to make the girls come. Then the boys attack the girls, and the boy gets the fun and the girl gets the tack." (I thought: !)

As a writer, I appreciate (and have made frequent use of) my daughter's gift for metaphor. One year, when we waited too long to buy tickets for *The Nutcracker* and ended up with one seat separate from the rest, Lauren asked me, "Who has to sit in the lonely seat?" I got a whole short story, title and all, out of that one.

And now I've got a chance to use it again. On the long drive home to Iowa, all seats in our car were lonely. Three times I turned around to say something to her. Three times.

Ever since we got back, I've been playing the "ago game." Let's say it's Tuesday afternoon. What am I thinking? Three weeks ago (or four or many more, depending on when you read this), we were still on our way to Ithaca, stopping at a roadside stand in Ontario, buying peaches and tomatoes that we ate in the car. (We poured a little water on the sleeve of a Dad-plaid shirt and used it to wipe off the fruit.)

Or maybe it's Tuesday evening, when we were in Niagara Falls, gawking at the roaring water lit up by a battery of colored spotlights almost as amazing as the falls themselves. A little later, we were hoping that no one had seen us pay six Canadian dollars apiece to enter Louis Tussaud's Waxworks museum, where we discovered that Elizabeth I was a dead ringer for Meryl Streep.

On any Wednesday, I can tell you exactly how many weeks ago we Journeyed Under the Falls in yellow plastic bags shaped like ponchos, puddling through tunnels in the rock behind the falling water, stopping to stare at the occasional pencil-wide stream springing out of the wall like a leak in the dike, wondering if we should be worried about this. In the Table Rock Gift Shop, across the street from the falls, all the souvenir cups and china knickknacks tinkled on their glass shelves, set to chattering by the pounding of the water.

On Thursday, Lauren showed us around the campus she had visited earlier in the year. We ate lunch on a veranda that boasts a view of half of New York state. That evening, in Watkins Glen, across the street from the rustic motel where we were staying, we walked through an arch in a wall of rock at the end of a parking lot and found ourselves in a magnificent gorge. For close to an hour we climbed up through layers of rock carved into waves and heart-shaped pools by the stream that drops through the middle of it all. We might have been on another continent, if not on another planet: all that strangeness and beauty on the other side of the street.

If we could just return to that Thursday, I keep thinking, and never get to Friday, for on Friday we waited in a line of cars, helpfully directed by a host of kids in red T-shirts to Lauren's dormitory, where it took only minutes to get all her stuff out of our car, which is to say, out of our life and into the next stopping place in hers.

On Saturday, any Saturday, I know exactly how many weeks ago we woke up without Lauren in our knotty-pine motel room, all too aware that today was the day we would leave without her. Packing up, I felt a burst of nostalgia for the *Cheers* reruns we'd watched together on a TV suspended hospital-style from the motel ceiling. Even the mismatched wallpaper and metal shower stall acquired a sudden charm.

"Looks like Rhinelander!" Lauren had said (four days ago) when we first opened the door.

The room took all of us back to Werner's Wonder Resort in Rhinelander, Wisconsin, August 1989. Ten years ago, all three of our kids were just the right age to thrill at the prospect of sleeping under the eaves of a knotty-pine cabin called The Blue Danube. Ten years ago, in the evening, after the waterskiing and tubing died down for the day, we listened for loons on the lake. Lauren, who was eight, got up by herself every morning, feeling like a big kid, and joined her Uncle Rick and his dog on the beach. Those were the days when a gloomy vacation sky once led her to remark, "If it would just begin to shine up, we'd all be happy immediately!"

Rhinelander was a great vacation—better than Disneyworld, the kids used to say—but what I'm remembering now is the Saturday morning that we left. It was raining. Ours was one in a long row of cars heading south, while in the northbound lane, another row of cars carried the families who would take our places in The Blue Danube and other cabins on the lakes of northern Wisconsin. We were all feeling a little blue as we inched along, when suddenly I felt something like panic, so desperately did I long to go back to the beginning of the week instead of coming to its end. I remember the wiper blades squeaking and me thinking—it was an odd moment to be sure—that this was what death would feel like: watching those other lucky folks go on without you, crying, Wait! Wait! I'm not finished yet! Give me one more day!

But that was ten years ago. Since then I've sent three kids off to college, and now I recognize that panic for what it is. Not quite so dire as death impending, it's just the way you feel before your youngest daughter runs up the granite steps and out of sight.

ON BABY WATCH

Waiting to Take the Plunge

From the end of September through mid-October, I was
on baby watch in Omaha, waiting to get the call from my
daughter that told me it was time. My part was to stay
with David, who's two, while Liz and Van went to the hospital
to bring forth his baby sister. Baby watch required that I leave
my cell phone on at all times, much to the amusement of my
students, who now know exactly how few calls I get. (*No wonder
she makes us turn ours off, poor thing!*) Faculty members who found
themselves in meetings interrupted by the jazzy riff of my ringtone may have been more annoyed than amused. Well, I'm sorry,
but I miss too many calls on "vibrate only." Besides, it's a great
ringtone. Sometimes I let it play a while before I pick up, though
not when I'm in a meeting.

Liz was due in October this time, and of course I'm going to
tell you how it all came out, but first let's flashback to early August 2010, when it was big bro David we were waiting for. The
first grandchild.

I was almost ready for one. My husband and I talked about it
one night in City Park pool, where we spend as much time as we
can every summer. I said I was worried.

"What's to worry about? A little *baby*," my husband cooed,
making a boat of his arms and rocking them on the water. (My
husband is a little weird. That's why I married him.) We had
paid three dollars extra to "Swim under the Stars" between 8:00
and 10:00 p.m. John went off the high dive for the occasion. I'd
watched him from here, waist deep.

"What if I forget his birthday?" I said, as if that were the problem.

"You won't," John said. He tilted his head sideways to knock the water out of his ear. "This is why I don't do that"—diving, he meant—"anymore."

"Swim under the Stars" was a fundraiser for the aquatic program. It was sponsored by Old Capitol City Roller Girls, which is a combination athletic team and charitable foundation. They donate a portion of the proceeds from every roller derby bout—that's what they call them—and from other fundraising events, such as the "Swim," to various local organizations and causes.

John and I knew very little about the Old Capitol City Roller Girls and their causes. We just wanted a chance to swim in that lovely pool on a warm summer night under the lights, something we used to do quite regularly, in the days before the pool's closing time rolled back from 9:00 to 8:00 p.m. We had come earlier for lap swim, and now we were lolling around in the water, treading and floating and watching the belly flop contest in the diving well. (There really was a contest. Those Roller Girls!) The belly floppers were mostly elementary and middle school kids, doing their best to make their friends and siblings shriek and their parents wince.

Those kids weren't trying to take my breath away at the thought of our three children, once this age and poised with their father on all four diving boards, having juggled their places in line so they could be the Flying Stefaniaks together. I used to watch them (and wince) from the shallow end.

Where did they go, those three children? That was the problem. *Where did they go?*

One of them was in Omaha at that very moment, counting down the days to her due date, which happened to be one week before her own birthday. (Now we both know, my daughter and I, what it's like to be due in August.)

Liz is our middle child, a Flying Stefaniak who always claimed the high dive. Ever the adventurer, she herself was a bottom-first breech birth. Can you picture one of those Olympic divers grasping her ankles as she tumbles off the platform, folded in half, somersaulting toward the water far below? That was Liz, minus the somersault, plummeting from womb to air with her ankles next to her ears. I'd tried to warn my obstetrician earlier that month that she felt heads-up to me, but what did I know, a curly-headed twenty-seven-year-old about to have her second baby? *He* was the Chief of Obstetrics at a major Milwaukee hospital. Did I know how many babies *he'd* delivered? Luckily, *I* was the Chief of Monster Contractions. Liz came right out into the world without so much as a helping pair of forceps. Given her position, my husband could yell on the very first push, "It's a girl!"

"No way they'd let you do that nowadays," Liz told me. "I'd have been a C-section for sure."

"They x-rayed us, quick, to see if you'd fit."

"They wouldn't do that either," she said.

They didn't have to, not this time. The grandson had his head down, ready to go. David Arthur Huett arrived, a Goliath-sized nine pounds thirteen ounces, just two days after he was due.

It was the first day of school at Creighton. Liz called me that morning to say she'd had some monster contractions of her own and she and Van were on their way to the hospital. The hospital wasn't far from campus. I figured I could make a dash to see the baby as soon as I got word. All day I waited for word. They're busy, I kept telling myself. I tried to concentrate on grading policies and other preparations for my four-hour class that night. World Literature: Beginnings to 1650. We're talking Gilgamesh to Shakespeare. On the syllabus for the first night were ancient Egyptian Love Poems (circa 1290 BCE) and a three-thousand-year-old collection of poems on all possible subjects called *The Chinese Book of Songs*. There was even a poem for the occasion,

#238, about Chiang Yuan, legendary mother of the Zhou people. Under the circumstances, I especially liked these lines:

> Indeed she had fulfilled her months,
> And her first-born came like a lamb
> With no bursting or rending,
> With no hurt or harm . . .
> That easily she bore her child.

Liz called back—*finally!*—at 5:30 p.m. My four-hour class was scheduled to begin at 5:45.

This is where my colleague Dr. Brooke Stafford (now Kowalke) enters the tale as my personal hero. She gets all the credit—as well as my undying gratitude—for offering to cover my class that night. "No way you're going to wait till tomorrow to see that baby," she said, and setting aside whatever plans she had for the evening, she pedaled back down to campus so that one first-time grandmother could hold her grandson in her arms on the very first evening of his life.

Two years, one month, and twenty-one days later, my baby watch duties came happily to an end when David's little sister, Vanessa Elizabeth Huett, plunged headfirst into the world—making a perfectly executed entry, as befits the daughter of a Flying Stefaniak.

IN A CLASS
BY ITSELF

WHO CARES, ANYWAY?

Diary of a School Age Romantic

by Mary Helen and Liz Stefaniak

I t was my friend Mori's husband who gave me the best com-
pliment ever. Having become a regular reader of my little essays, Tony once remarked, "How much fun she has in her life!
Then she writes it all down, and I get to enjoy it too."

He was right. I do have fun in my life — now. Not so in years
past, I'm afraid. If Tony had peeked at my grade school diary, he
would have agreed that "Life sure is dull for a 12-year-old" (noted
Sept. 29, 1963). In those days, I wrote down things like movies
I'd watched on the *Late Show* and problems with my homework
(that first-aid booklet troubled me for weeks), along with laments
over parties I didn't get invited to and reports that Rocky (our
dog) "'went' on the stairs." The only exciting entry describes the
day the Beatles left Milwaukee. Judene and I were at the Air National Guard hangars to see them off:

> Sept. 5, 1964
> We were so close to the road, and the limosine [sic] had to
> slow down to turn toward the airplane. PAUL LEANED
> OVER BY THE WINDOW AND WAVED TO US.
> He looked right at us (where we were it wasn't crowded) and
> we looked at him.

A glorious moment of eye contact, to be sure, but not typical.
Far more common are entries like this one.

Oct. 25, 1964
Dear Diary,

This writing is funny because I'm holding the pencil oddly. My hand is sore from working on my first aid booklet.

Let's return to events of the fun-filled present, like the last time my daughter Liz came home for a visit. I was nodding off at the computer at about 1:30 a.m. when I heard raucous laughter overhead. I went upstairs and found my twenty-one-year-old daughter lying on my bed, reading her fifth-to-eighth grade diary. "Oh my god, Mom," she gasped. "Listen to this."

We laughed until our stomachs hurt. At 2:30 my husband came home from a band gig and all three of us laughed until well after 3:00 in the morning.

Now I don't claim that my daughter's experiences were those of your typical ten-to-thirteen-year-old, nor that she had more or less fun than other girls her age. The entries we found funniest don't exactly chart a sexual awakening (for God's sake, she was only twelve years old!), but they do suggest her growing self-consciousness in relation to boys. In this, she was way ahead of me. The only boys mentioned with interest in my diary at age twelve are John, Paul, George, and Ringo.

Printed here, with her permission, are excerpts from Elizabeth's diary—incomplete and somewhat expurgated, the names having been changed to protect the innocence of everybody but the poor author herself. Some language may be unsuitable for children twelve and under, but that's life.

Growing up is one thing. Writing it all down is another. I confess it gives me pause to think that Liz wrestled with questions of dating and kissing (and worse!) at an age when I was still playing with doll houses or, a little later, papering my walls with pictures of the Beatles. On the other hand, like Tony, I'm glad she wrote it all down so we can enjoy it too.

Fifth Grade

Thurs., Oct. 13, 1988
Dear Diary,

Today a hot-shot fifth grader named Brian Johnson got stuck inside his locker. They don't have locks, but his handle was broken. He kept screaming, "Let me out!" He thought someone was holding him in. Then Mr. Davis walked by, and we told Brian to shut up. He did, and people made quick conversation. Sara finally got him out with a fingernail. I have a viola lesson today.

Tues., Oct. 18, 1988
Dear Diary,

Today I have MORE HOMEWORK! It's driving me CRAZY! Ug. I found a new way to style my bangs. It's cool. We played kickball in recess today. It was fun, even if my team lost.

Sat., Dec. 17, 1988
Dear Diary,

This past week I had patrol in the morning and afternoon. It was COLD! Today I'm having a Christmas party and I have a lot of cleaning to do. Then I have to make cookies. Jon Cartwright is really cute. If he weren't such a jerk, I could actually like him. He hasn't done anything jerky for a while, though. I think he's getting nicer. I hope so 'cause he's awfully cute. Right now I have three presents for me under the tree.

Mon., Feb. 27, 1989
Dear Diary,

The Hancher concert was great. Two people left the stage because of faintness and illness. After the concert we went to dinner at Jon's house. I had a great time. Jon says he's going to grow his hair to his shoulders. I hope he doesn't. He's one of the cutest guys I've ever seen, and it might ruin his looks.

Sixth Grade

Mon., Oct. 9, 1989
Dear Diary,

I think I might be in love. I didn't meet this guy, I saw him in a play. His name is Randy Hanson. He's a sophomore at West, I think, and he is so cute!!!!!!! I will never see him again, probably. Oh, well.

Sun., Oct. 15, 1989
Dear Diary,

I think this bizness with Randy isn't love. This happens to me when I see somebody who's really cute. Who cares, anyway?

Seventh Grade

Fri., Sept. 7, 1990
Dear Diary,

Oh, my god! Holy s—t, you will not believe this! Nick Shea just called me and asked me to go to a movie Saturday at 4:00. AAAAAAAH!!!!!!!!!! A date! My god, my first date, and—of all people—with Nick. Man, you're supposed to go on dates with OTHER guys, not your friends. I gotta call Jessica as soon as Dad gets off the phone. Anyway, WOW!

P.S. Mom said I couldn't date until I was in high school. Oh, well, it's just Nick. She has nothing to fear because he's my friend.

Thurs., Dec. 20, 1990

Dear Diary,

Ah, life is becoming easier to handle now that I'm going with Dustin. I can't wait until tomorrow, because I get to ush [sic] at the play. What should I wear? (It has to be perfect.) Dustin said he'd french me if I wanted him to, and Esther and Jessica think I'm a baby, but I don't want to be frenched! A kiss I can handle (and am looking forward to), but frenching? For God's sake, I'm only 12 years old! Geez, you guys! Give it up!

Fri., Dec. 28, 1990

Dear Diary,

I told Dustin I didn't want him to french me and he wasn't mad or offended at all. (Jessica was disappointed.)

Eighth Grade

Sat., April 11, 1992

Dear Diary,

The dance was last night. It was fun. I asked Jason if it would piss him off if I asked him not to dance with other people. He said, "Noooo, but it might piss some other people off. Would it piss you off if I did?" I said, yeah, kind of. So he wasn't going to. I hope it didn't piss him off.

Who cares, anyway?

ROLE MODELS

INFREQUENT FLIER

Airborne in the Dairy Section

JANUARY 1998

When you're walking around town with a bright pink cast on your arm, people ask you, "How did it happen?" I've been tempted to give a rueful "yes" to the ones who say, "Don't tell me—you were rollerblading?" but the truth is more mundane and more ominous. After all, we expect sticks and stones (and rollerblades) to break our bones. All I needed was a bit of spilled milk on the floor in front of the dairy case.

It happened in the supermarket formerly known as Econofoods on September 1, as I was reaching over to pick up a gallon of milk. A fellow shopper in the yogurt area witnessed my fall. He described it for me later.

"You leaned over to pick up the milk and as you picked it up, your weight must have shifted, and your one foot flew out from under you, and then your other foot came up after it, and you threw both your hands up into the air so that the milk went one way and the basket"—a plastic one with metal handles that contained, among other things, a carton of extra large eggs—"went the other."

"Wait a minute," I said. "Do you mean to say I was *airborne*?"

"You were airborne!"

While airborne, I must have twisted around somehow because I landed with my back to the dairy case in a small but spreading lake of milk. I had tried to catch myself in what would have been a one-point landing and actually heard the humble snap of what turned out to be my radial bone breaking. When it was all over,

I was holding my left wrist in my right hand, saying out loud, in amazement, after a couple of unprintables, "I think I broke my arm!" This was a good guess. My left arm looked like an S-shaped curve. It also hurt like—well, like the dickens.

Enter Ansa Akyea, the aforementioned witness, a University of Iowa graduate student in theatre arts, who recognized good improv when it landed at his feet. With a growing audience of customers and employees, including one with a mop and one with a clipboard, Ansa sat down beside me in the puddle of milk and set up a steady stream of talk to distract me from my S-shaped arm. He also let me lean against him to keep from falling over. He was perfect for the part. He was better than *ER*.

"Look at me," he said. "Don't look at your arm—look at me!"

"I broke my arm," I told him.

"What's your name?" he said.

I told him that, too.

"Okay, Mary, look at me now. My name is Ansa."

"It's what?"

"Ansa."

"What?"

"Ansa. Ansa. Like 'answer.'"

"Ansa," I said—or maybe I said "Answer."

"Yes! Now. Look at me, Mary. Are you here by yourself?"

I was. I had a car with a stick shift and no power steering out in the parking lot. It was a cute little car, a Volvo 1800ES vintage 1973 sports hatchback with an all-glass rear door. In Europe they call them "Snow White's Coffin."

"Is there someone we can call?" he asked.

My daughter, I said. Ansa beckoned to a hovering employee, then turned back to me.

"So. Tell me, Mary. What did you come to the store to buy? Don't look at it. Look at me. What did you come to buy?"

"Just something for supper," I said mournfully. "We were going to eat out. We should have eaten out."

"So!" Ansa was brisk, showing no patience for useless hindsight. "What were you going to make for supper?"

"What?"

"For supper," he said, with feeling. "What were you going to make?"

"Fried rice," I moaned.

"Ah! Fried rice—look at me—and what do you need to make fried rice?"

"Rice," I wailed.

I was not at my best conversationally, but Ansa kept me talking until a friendly fireman from the rescue squad took over, freeing Ansa to answer the clipboard's questions and finally to return to a little boy—his cousin, it turned out—who was patiently waiting in the wings. By the time the ambulance arrived and they put me on the gurney and rolled me through the store like a float in the homecoming parade, Ansa and his cousin were gone. I'd neglected to ask what they were planning to have for supper. Whatever it was, it must have been late.

Our big scene was over, but the worst of a broken wrist was yet to come. First, of course, the bone had to be set—a procedure that's like a cross between arm wrestling and a tug of war, except that one opponent is stretched out on a table, arm in the air, and the other is standing with both feet braced firmly on the floor. Then came weeks of inconvenience: I couldn't type or even write worth a darn (except with my right hand on very large pieces of cardboard); I couldn't drive my little car; I couldn't eat soup in public; I couldn't have my daily swim. (On the other hand, I couldn't wash the dishes.) When the cast finally came off, my left hand was a stranger to me: a narrow, hairy fan of a hand merging vaguely into a thick wrist. Nobody knows, apparently, why a temporary coat of dark hair develops under the cast. It is one of the remaining mysteries of the universe.

What did I learn from my experience? That we are breakable creatures and that the world is a slippery and dangerous place.

I knew that already, of course, but now I knew it in a way that made my knees weak when I approached the dairy case. I also learned—and here's the silver lining—that people like Ansa Akyea are out there in the dangerous world, sure of their lines and ready to be leaned on.

POSTSCRIPT 2020: Ansa Akyea finished graduate school, earning his MFA at the University of Iowa, and went on to an acting career spanning more than twenty years (so far) in films, TV, and on the stage. I wish I could say that I followed his career over the years, but the truth is that I looked him up just now. I recognized him in this description, published in *City Pages* in Minneapolis, when he was named Actor of the Year: "Ansa Akyea brings a combination of dramatic heft and humane lightness to every role he touches. While he isn't particularly tall, he has such a physical presence that he could pass for a six-plus-footer. And he's blessed with a big, expressive, handsome mug that enables him to run the gamut from heartthrob to nurturing protector." I can't attest to his height since he crouched beside me in the puddle of milk throughout our big scene, and intense brown eyes are the only feature of his handsome mug that I remember clearly. ("Look at me! Don't look at your arm—look at me!") What I recognize in the description are the "dramatic heft and humane lightness" that he brought to the role of "nurturing protector" in Econofoods that day, a role he played so convincingly opposite my "injured shopper" that I can only believe it was one of those cases where the actor is playing himself.

REMEMBERING ELLEN

The Porridge Club Never Forgets

· JULY 1998

This is what I learned from my good friend Ellen Hickerson—teacher, swimmer, bibliophile, octogenarian, gourmand du chocolat, and all around bonne vivante. I learned that no matter what may be in store for me in the future, no matter what kinds of things happen, even terrible things like blindness and crippling arthritis and the loss of people I love, I don't have to be diminished by them. Challenged, yes, saddened, but not diminished. No matter what happens, like Ellen, I can keep growing. There's always something new to try, something to learn.

She taught me this, of course, by her example. I met Ellen in the rec center locker room in 1991, and in the seven years I disrobed, suited up, and showered beside her, I've never known her to be so dull as to deliver an uplifting lecture—although she might offer an interesting opinion on the origins of the Peloponnesian Wars or the contributions of Hegel to contemporary thought. In the last three years of her life, after her failing eyesight introduced her to the Talking Books program of the Iowa Department for the Blind, Ellen became (if she wasn't already) the best-read person in Iowa City. She sometimes listened to two or three books a day. The Talking Books audio player came with variable listening speeds.

It's hard to describe Ellen without giving you the wrong idea about her. I could try to convey how strong and brave she was by cataloging her losses—not only her arthritis and fading vision, but the broken hip, the broken arm, a host of "minor" ailments, and a parade of loved ones lost that stretches back to the death of her mother when Ellen was only four. If I do that, you might think, "That poor woman."

Believe me. Among those who knew Ellen Hickerson—including the fifth graders at Hoover Elementary who read and discussed the newspaper with her every week—no one ever thought of her as "that poor woman."

If I describe her physically? Same problem. You're apt to picture a frail old lady taking small, slow steps with the help of a four-footed metal cane, her white hair swept up under a knit cap or a terrycloth turban, and her wide, blue eyes getting wider and bluer as the world darkened for her. Though accurate in detail, this description also misses Ellen by a mile.

So here's a story. In 1994, Ellen decided that she couldn't see well enough to drive anymore. She engaged the Johnson County SEATS bus to bring her to the pool instead. (One day, when the bus couldn't maneuver through construction to get her to the rec center door, she had the driver drop her off at the Greyhound station in the next block and took a taxi the rest of the way.) Picture her coming into the locker room four mornings a week, her purple swim bag slung over her shoulder and her metal cane at her side, full of praise and stories about those considerate, *interesting* SEATS drivers—this one a model train aficionado, that one a grower of organic tomatoes. They know just how to respond to the problems of the novice rider, Ellen says. One morning she reports, "I couldn't get my seatbelt buckled today, so I said to the driver, 'I'm having a little trouble with my seatbelt.' When that young woman turned around, she saw immediately what the problem was. She said, 'Ma'am, that's the fire extinguisher.'"

You have to picture Ellen—and the variously undressed crowd around her—hooting with laughter at this story.

Okay. Now imagine her sitting on the bench, fully clothed and waiting for me to finish fussing with my makeup so that we can join our Porridge Club friends for breakfast after our Saturday swim. Patiently, she offers me a cracker from the stash in her coat pocket and with only a hint of irony, observes, "You know, now that I can't see my face in the mirror, I can put my lipstick on anywhere."

And how did she describe for us the carrot cake she made for her grandson's graduation?

"Let me put it this way," she said. "Everyone could tell that it was definitely homemade."

I think we're getting closer now to who she was.

She liked chocolate better than anything. She could name fine chocolatiers around the world, and when someone sent her a gift box, she was not above hiding it to savor what remained after the family and an intimate friend or two had had their taste. (I once helped her pick fuzz off chocolates that had slipped out of a box hidden between her washer and dryer.) I also remember a night at the Linn Street Cafe when Ellen ordered a kind of double dark frosted fudge cake, which came on a white plate artistically drizzled with chocolate. I won't say that Ellen licked the drizzles off her plate after she finished her dessert. I *will* say that when the waitress came to take the plates, there was no chocolate left on Ellen's.

The woman knew how to live.

She drew people like a magnet. Strangers could feel her generosity, her delight in their presence, her certainty that everyone was worth her while. As we dripped and dried one Saturday, a fellow swimmer brought her three-year-old over to show him off to Ellen, or maybe vice versa, instructing him to shake the nice lady's hand. When Ellen held out her skinny arm and bony, age-spotted fingers, I saw for a moment how they might look to a three-year-old, and I worried. I should have known better. Like everyone else, the little boy felt Ellen's aura, and he reached up shyly, grinning at her from behind his towel. (Ellen confided later, "That's the first time I've ever been introduced to a young man while I was completely naked." Actually, she had a towel on her head.)

The last three days of Ellen's life went like this. On Tuesday, she went swimming. It was sunny, and she hung her suit outside to dry. On Wednesday, she fell ill. When I went to see her in the ICU, she took my hand and said, "Oh, Mary Helen, I'm so glad you came. You can tell the others we won't be having porridge at my house this Saturday." I thought right away of porridge delivered hot to the hospital—*Party in Ellen's room!*—but on Thursday, surrounded by her family, Ellen died.

The locker room seems awfully empty now, without her black shoes waiting under the bench.

When my firstborn went off to college a few years ago, Ellen gave me some good advice. She said, "You can cry in the pool if you need to. Nobody will see your tears." We're keeping this in mind as we learn to live without her.

SATURDAYS WITH SARAH

What We Learned from Our Friend

MAY 2000

O ur dear friend Sarah Lamb, cofounder of the Porridge Club, died on Monday, April 3, of complications from ALS, a neuromuscular disease that had whittled away at her body for three years but left her spirit untouched. It takes considerable strength of character to come through loud and clear when you can hardly raise your eyebrows for "yes" or close your eyes for "no." Sarah came through loud and clear.

The exact date is lost in the mists of the early 1990s, but we do know that on the Saturday morning when Sarah Lamb joined Ellen Hickerson and me at the Hamburg Inn after swimming and informed us in her crisp Yorkshire accent that it was porridge, not oatmeal, we were eating with our nuts and raisins, on that day, Porridge Club was born. Membership and meeting place have varied over the years, moving from the Burg to one another's houses and finally settling at Mori's place, next door to Sarah's, where we met to eat and talk almost every Saturday. Most of us continue to uphold our motto: "First we swim. Then we eat."

As one of our founders, Sarah took her Porridge Club membership seriously. When she could no longer swim, she came to eat and talk. And when she could no longer eat or talk, she came to listen, to smell the food, and to put in her two cents' worth by Dynamyte (her talking computer) or eyebrow. Sarah attended her last Porridge Club meeting, where she enjoyed whiffs of asparagus tempura, roasted veggies with hummus, and triple-threat chocolate cookies (the menu has evolved) the Saturday before she died. The way I see it, she and Ellen Hickerson now constitute our first chapter in the hereafter. I hope that they're having a good time together, that the water is fine, and that the showers are hot and stay on long enough.

There's something about swimmers, I guess. My daughter Elizabeth (an occasional swimmer herself) once said that, because we knew Ellen Hickerson, we know how to live to a ripe old age without ever getting old. Having known Sarah, we know how to live with the worst possible physical limitations, how to lose the ability to do one thing after another—swimming a lap, eating a meal, making a phone call—without ever giving up who we are, without ever letting go of life. You could also say, although no one likes to use the word, that Sarah taught us how to die.

Here, as far as I can tell, is how you do it: you just keep on living till the end. You don't become a hero; you don't become a saint or a paragon of wisdom (although in a sense Sarah was all those things). You stay who you are.

The things that annoy you (lukewarm coffee, throwing away recyclables, silverware in the wrong drawers), still annoy you. The things that make you laugh (like your pair of hefty cats, those "solid citizens"), still make you laugh. You dream of chocolate. You refuse to be "confined" by your wheelchair. You take your daily constitutional in the jogger, an adult-sized stroller a.k.a. the Sarahmobile, often rolling down to the river. You feed the ducks. On Sunday you go out to West Branch Friends Church, where, I'm sure, you take a moment to remind God that you're still here, still Sarah, that you're trying hard not to feel buried alive lately, and you could use a little help with that. God, it would seem, comes through for you. So do the Friends, who line up to chat with you after meeting and sign-up in great numbers to bring you soup and other forms of sustenance.

You go to town meetings and political rallies. You get your picture in the paper chumming it up with the candidate, who happens to be Bill Bradley. You greet the admiring public in Happy Hollow Park at the start and finish of the PALS 5K run that you and your sons have organized to fight the disease that you never give in to, no matter what it takes away.

You go to New Zealand with those two fine sons. You see them swim with the dolphins.

You accept no visitors when *Mystery* or *Masterpiece Theater* is on. Your friends take you to concerts and plays. (You forgive them when they can't figure out that you need your glasses to see the stage.)

When you have something to say, you say it, no matter how long it takes to adjust the switch on the Dynamyte so the smallest pressure from your knee will select the right row, then the right letter, to build one word, then another, until your sentence is ready to be spoken. (You sound like Stephen Hawking!)

Often, the conversation has moved on without you, but you forgive your friends for speaking so fluently. At Porridge Club, when you ask for some quiche and the little machine voice says, "May I please try the kwichee?" you laugh. You play it again.

Later, you ask only to smell the quiche and the chocolate cheesecake, and you forgive your friends for eating them. It gets harder and harder to raise your eyebrows for yes, but you try your best to do it anyway. When others misunderstand, you forgive them. Sometimes you weep with frustration. When your friends can't tell if you're laughing or crying, you forgive them. When you want to give somebody a good, swift kick, you forgive yourself.

You forgive—but you don't give in. You hold out for what you want, what you need. There's still so much to enjoy, after all, so much to be thankful for. You can still light up with pleasure when the children across the street come by to say hello or sing a song or show you something. When you're rolling down Brown Street toward the sunset and the river, you can still feel the wind caressing your face. When someone gets you settled just right in your chair, or wheels you past a crowd of crocuses, or holds a sprig of lilac to your nose; when Zeb the cat leaps into your lap; when your son sits down to read or watch TV where you can feast your eyes on him — at those times you're still amazed to be in a world that has such beauty in it.

The truth is, Sarah, you did not teach us how to live or die with a catastrophic illness. You taught us, simply, how to live. You taught us how to recognize important moments, like this one, which I jotted down in my notebook not three months after we learned of your diagnosis:

June 25, 1997. This morning a few of us went to the Hamburg Inn after our swim. Sarah happened by on her way to help serve lunch at Wesley House just as Mori, Ellen, and I had come out the door of the Burg. Later, Sarah told me she wished she had a camera to take our picture out there on the sidewalk, Mori in her red top, me in my blue flowered dress, Ellen in her black and white striped blouse. "You looked so wonderful," Sarah said, "so refreshed and bright and happy."

FROM THE LOCKER ROOM

Living Your Life in Technicolor

Sometimes the world goes gray on you. Fuzzy. The details blur. The colors fade. You check your glasses, but that doesn't seem to be the problem. (The letters on the computer screen, the figures on your bank statement—these are all too clear.) No, this is a haziness of the soul, a featureless fog in which you can see all your tomorrows creeping in their petty pace through week after week, looking as gray as the March sky outside your window.

I know I've got them—not the blues, but the grays—when I can't come up with anything to think about while I swim, which is when I do much of my best thinking, or when I look through my notebook and find I haven't written down a wacky bit of conversation or even a heartfelt description of the sunrise in more than a week. I had to page all the way back to mid-January to find something better than "sun appears at 7:55" or "Omaha squirrels like apples more than corn."

What I found was a conversation overheard in the locker room on campus. (Being a swimmer, I spend a lot of time in locker rooms.) One young woman was telling another that her mother was worried that she'd "forget where she came from" after she graduated and got married and started making her share of a quarter of a million dollars a year. I don't know what field she was studying, but just by the way she said, "Jim and I's combined salary," I could tell that she wasn't an English major.

Being an English teacher myself, I knew this evidence of my irrelevance in the great money-making scheme of things was not what I needed to pull me out of the doldrums. So I kept looking until I found another locker room conversation, also in January, this one with a little girl at Mercer Park pool in Iowa City. Dark-haired, skinny, and wet, she was walking ahead of me out of the showers, each of us wrapped in a towel, when I said, "Brrrr."

She looked up at me over her shoulder and asked, "What did you say?"

"I'm freezing," I told her. By now we were at the bench in front of our respective lockers, which were, following the natural law of locker selection in an otherwise empty locker room, side by side. I asked her if she was cold. She said she wasn't. I told her she was lucky.

"Well," she said, letting her towel slip off her shoulders to reveal a leopard skin swimsuit. "I was in the hot tub for a long time, you see, and then I had a warm shower."

We dried and dressed in silence for a while. I was about half finished when she asked, "How old are you?"

It was not a prying question but a conversation starter.

"Oh, I'm *old*," I said, just like a grown-up. I thought she looked a little disappointed in me, so I quickly asked, "How old are *you?*"

"Six," she said.

"Well," I said, shamed by her forthrightness, "I'm *forty*-six."

When she opened her mouth wide in astonishment, I could see that her two front teeth were missing on top and just starting to grow in on the bottom. "That has a six, too!" she said. She looked pleased about this as she buttoned and zipped. After a while she offered, "My birthday is the same as my grandpa's. It's March 5."

I pointed out that it was coming up very soon. She happily agreed. Then she asked, "So is it your birthday today?"

"No," I said. "But it *is* in January."

Her whole face lit up with joy for me. She said, "*This* is January!"

Basking in the glow of my good fortune, we continued our locker room business. She was still smiling to herself when

I pulled my boots out of the locker and stood them beside the bench.

"Whoa, those are tall boots!" she said. "You can really walk in the snow in those."

She paused in the course of putting a pink and white boot on her own foot and chopped the top of her thigh with the side of her hand. "The snow by our house is up to *here* on me," she said. "The snowplows made mountains."

She marked the place on her pink sweatpants again. "I'll bet your boots would come up to here on me."

"I think they would."

"I bet they're good where it's drifted," she said.

I said they were.

She was all dressed now and mentioned, in case I was interested, that she would be back at the pool for a birthday party on Sunday. Then she left the locker room, lost in a big navy-blue nylon parka with a fake fur–trimmed hood.

A few minutes later, I was walking out to the car when I noticed that the little girl was walking many steps behind me. (She was completely absorbed in unwrapping a candy bar, her face hidden by the hood of her parka.) From the car, I called good-bye to her. She looked up from her candy bar long enough to wave. I was about to tell my husband about her when he looked out the window and said, to my surprise, "That little girl is an unusual child."

His story about her was better than mine. It seems he had been in the hot tub one time with the little girl in the leopard skin suit. At Mercer Park, the hot tub is a rectangle about ten feet long by eight feet wide and forty inches deep. She and another little girl were moving from place to place between the bubbling spouts in the sides of the hot tub, talking about which places were their lucky spots to sit. The little girl in the leopard skin suit ended up between two bubbling spouts with my husband in the corner to the left of her and another man — the only other person in the hot tub — to her right.

"This is my luckiest spot," the little girl told her friend. When the friend asked why, she answered, "Because I'm sitting between two brave men."

John and the other man looked at each other over the top of her head, but all they saw was an ordinary guy on the other side of the hot tub, middle-aged and wet.

"She must have been telling herself a story in her head," John said to me in the car.

That's where the entry in my notebook ends, but sitting here at my desk with gray sky and melting snow outside the window, I can picture her adventures like a movie. A little girl in hip boots drives a team of huskies — no, of leopards — through a blizzard across mountains of snow, those two brave men in sleds beside her. Or maybe they're firefighters, the three of them, climbing ladders and wielding hoses to rescue Grandpa from the inferno ignited by the multitude of candles on his birthday cake.

Whatever the story in her head, you can bet that it played in Technicolor. No gray days for this child, not when there's a drama in every hot tub, a story behind every face — and anyone's birthday is cause for joy.

TRAVELS

I LOVE NEW YORK

A Cornhusking, Cheese-Headed Hawkeye
Bites the Big Apple

MAY 2001

Until recently, I guess I had a midwesterner's idea of New York City. It was a cold, indifferent place, where faceless millions prey upon each other in their struggle to survive. Although I personally knew two New Yorkers who did not fit this profile, I assumed they were exceptions to the rule.

What can I say? I'm a midwesterner, no matter how you look at it. I was born in Wisconsin, and grew up there, raised my children in Iowa City, and now I teach in Omaha, Nebraska. When I was asked to speak at a conference at Columbia University in March of 2001, I almost said no, daunted by the thought of being alone in New York City.

My New York experience began with my Chicago-to-LaGuardia flight, which was cancelled. This, I learned, was very New York, very LaGuardia. I bounced from gate to gate in search of another flight, worked my way from the bottom to very near the top of two different stand-by lists, and finally got a seat on a three o'clock flight that was cleared to take off at 4:30. On this flight, at 4:30, a speaker crackled and the pilot said, "Folks, there's no good way to tell you this." Something hydraulic was broken, and we had to return to the terminal instead of taking off.

While passengers up and down the aisles groaned about yet another delay, I met my first New Yorker of the trip. Joseph Levy, a hardware store impresario from Brooklyn, who had the window seat beside me, turned to me and said, "Better they should find it now than later."

I agreed, heartily.

Next, Joseph Levy reached down and plucked a plastic grocery store sack from the big nylon gym bag open at his feet. "A long time we've been on this plane already," he said. "My wife and my mother both make food for me." He hefted the sack. "It's too much. I can't eat it all. Here, if you get hungry, it's yours."

I wondered politely if food would be served on the flight.

"Oh," he said, "I don't eat that airplane food. I've been to the plant. Here, take something. I got candy—you're sure you don't want anything? If you get hungry, don't even ask. Don't ask. Just help yourself. Just like you're at home. Better you should eat it, and I don't make my teeth any worse than they already are."

He smiled broadly.

I tried to think of what ulterior motive Joseph Levy might have for offering candy to a stranger like me, but everything about him pointed to simple generosity. He discreetly made use of his cell phone while I rummaged through the sack. Once I'd found my candy bar, he flipped the phone shut and asked me if I'd ever heard of "Darattzappa." I hadn't. He said he'd just come from selling a pile of them in Milwaukee yesterday. I said I was from Milwaukee.

"No!" he said. "Really?"

He reached again into his gym bag and this time pulled out a blue plastic box with a toggle switch and a little red light on the top.

The Rat Zapper turned out to be a have-a-heart style trap with an electric floor plate inside (instead of a heart) to zap the rat, killing it painlessly in seconds, according to Joseph Levy. The current comes from just four C batteries and is perfectly safe for larger-than-rat-sized pets and children.

"There's no pain, no blood, no mouse or rat crying in the trap," Joseph Levy said. "The lady of the house doesn't even have to see the dead rat." She can just pick up the blue box and dump the rat out the open end. (Into what you dump a zapped rat, Joseph Levy didn't say.) Then she flips the switch on the top, the indicator light goes out, and the trap is ready to zap another rat.

If you'd like to know more about the Rat Zapper, by the way, you can go to www.ratzapper.com. I happen to know someone looking to hire a midwestern sales rep.

"This one's never been used," Joseph Levy added, slipping the blue box back into his gym bag.

When I told him I was going to spend four days in Manhattan, he looked worried. "Plenty of weirdos in Manhattan," he warned. He plucked a business card (featuring a cartoon rat) from his vest pocket and jotted his cell phone number on the back. "Just in case you run into trouble," he said.

All I ran into were more friendly strangers like him.

On my first night, way up in the thin air of a twenty-one-dollar balcony seat at Carnegie Hall, for example, I sat next to young Peter Wong, a music student at Brooklyn College, who introduced himself on the long climb back to our seats during intermission. Before the music started again, I was telling young Peter Wong that I taught at a university in far-off Omaha, Nebraska. A woman in the row in front of us turned around and guessed, correctly, "Creighton?" One of her best friends had graduated from there.

In the subway the next morning, while waiting for the wrong train, I asked a young woman who was waiting with me if this train would take me to 116th and Broadway. "Let's go down here to the map," she said, in a clipped Caribbean way. En route to the map, she nabbed another young woman for advice. When I said I was trying to get to Columbia University, they both cried, "Oh, Columbia!" Together, they walked me to the right stairs.

By my third day in Manhattan, the counter guy at the Universal News Café around the corner from my hotel knew what to put in my coffee before I asked. He got it sweet enough too. He was from Morocco.

I had other quick conferences on street corners and at bus

stops, sometimes three or four people gathering to debate the best route for getting me where I was going. Twice, people asked *me* for directions, and we joined forces to ask somebody else. When my daughter came down on the bus from Ithaca to spend Saturday with me in Manhattan, we met chatty taxi drivers and a gift shop clerk at the Metropolitan Museum of Art who woke up from a nap beside the cash register and cheerfully drew us a map to the Egyptian exhibit.

On Friday, my daughter and I had dinner with friends in their apartment on the twenty-third floor of a building on East 71st Street. (In the elevator, Lauren said, "I don't think I've ever been in a building this tall.") Amused by my tales of helpful New Yorkers, my friends said that I must be sending out some kind of wholesome greenhorn vibe that made people want to be nice to me.

Maybe. Or maybe New York is well supplied with people who know firsthand the value of smoothing the way for other strangers like themselves. Midwesterners sometimes like to say, "There are no strangers here — only friends we haven't met." Maybe, in Manhattan, you don't have to be friends. People recognize themselves in you even if you're a stranger.

Or maybe people could just tell how much I liked Manhattan, how happy I was to be there: all those buildings rising like a giant Legoland straight up out of the water, the long avenues like canyons with blue sky at either end. I liked walking on crowded sidewalks past Tiffany's and Carnegie Hall, down Fifth Avenue and through Times Square, waiting for a gap in the traffic at the corner, then surging across the street with the crowd to the sound of honking taxis. In my favorite photo from the trip (taken by my daughter), I'm windblown and grinning on the deck of the Liberty Island ferry, the whole of Manhattan behind me, the twin towers of the World Trade Center standing nearly twice as tall as every other building, like a pair of smokestacks rising amidships from the deck of the city.

Manhattan is an old-fashioned place, really. People walk, they take cabs and subways and the Madison Avenue bus. They're like characters in a story by Dorothy Parker or E. B. White, but with a lot more color in the mix. Some of them live on the twenty-third floor of buildings whose doormen will call upstairs to announce that Mary Helen is here.

TALES OF A HAPPY TRAVELER

From the Chunnel to Sunny Florida

FEBRUARY 2012

Wε had just returned from a week in Florida, and I was feeling a little sad as I read my notes about all the fun that was over now. Paging through my notebook, trying to remember exactly what we'd done each day, I came across something. It was a note I'd jotted before the trip about a psychology professor named Sonja Lyubomirsky, who had received a grant from the National Institute of Mental Health to conduct research on the possibility of permanently increasing happiness. She was talking about travel. "Trips aren't all perfect," she said, "but we remember them as perfect."

Do we? I thought. The trips that fill the most pages in my notebooks are the ones where things went wrong. If the trip you remember was perfect, you can be pretty sure that no one wants to hear about it. If it was a perfect disaster, you'll find everyone is all ears.

Just ask my husband about the time he accidentally left his computer bag at our departure gate when we boarded a plane in Detroit. We were already in our seats when John talked the flight attendant into letting him go back for it, escorted by appropriate personnel. This is a story that involves both airport security and the Detroit Police Department. It includes lines such as "Step away from the bag, sir!" and "No, you can't get back on the *plane*." Oh, and don't forget "How would you like to spend a night in the Detroit City Jail?"

When John tells this story—which wasn't a *perfect* disaster, since the bomb-sniffing dogs showed no interest in him or his computer bag, and in the end they let him get back on the plane—his audience is rapt.

Also riveting is the story of a "day trip" to Paris that John took on his own when I was teaching in Dublin one summer. His plan was to fly Ryanair to London, book a cheap hotel, and fulfill a long-held dream by taking the Chunnel train to Paris the following morning. After spending the day, he would ride the last train back to London and catch his flight the next morning to Dublin, where he would meet me for lunch at Trinity after my class.

The trip began with a delightful breakfast on the train. John had just consumed a croissant spread with jam *and* honey (from little jars of each), and he was emptying the flagon (his word) of coffee into his cup when the attendant came by with her cart and whisked away his tray to make room for the second course! John delved into sausage and eggs and fat tomato slices, all but beside himself with joy. After breakfast, the descent of the train into the Chunnel coincided perfectly with his own descent into dreamland.

Arriving at the Gard du Nord, he was undaunted by the rain—one of the ten French words he knows being, conveniently, the one for *umbrella*. He walked great distances in the rain, climbed the Eiffel Tower in the rain, sat in the rain where he and I once sat, under a different parapluie, on the quai at the tip of l'Île de la Cité. Then he walked back to the Gard du Nord. He found it strangely empty.

"Too late!" the station master told him in several languages. "Come tomorrow!"

Having forgotten that Paris and London are in different time zones, he had missed the last train.

Ask John and he'll tell you about walking from hotel to hotel in the pouring rain of a Paris evening, looking for one that wasn't booked solid by the influx of attendees at a weekend air show. Eventually, he had to pay for an expensive suite. He put on the fluffy white robe and hung his wet clothes on the radiators overnight. But here's the thing about my husband, a chronically happy traveler if ever there was one. By the time he was enjoying his second course on the first Chunnel train back to London, where he caught his 9:00 a.m. flight to Dublin and met me on time for lunch, he probably *was* remembering the whole trip as "perfect."

Professor Lyubomirsky has done other happiness research, by the way. On her website she mentions a recent study in which participants were asked to increase their level of happiness by "practicing optimism" or "expressing gratitude."

I have chosen to do the latter here, regarding our recent holiday trip to Florida.

I am grateful to my daughter Liz and her husband, Van, for accepting the almost impossible mission of flying with a sixteen-month-old child. Traveling with David required his faithful retainers to tote three checked bags, a folding bed, a stroller, a car seat, a backpack (baby food, diapers, etc.), and a "mystery bag" of new toys to delight and distract. At least they didn't have to carry a book or magazine, you know, to read on the plane.

I am grateful to David for being overwhelmed with delight by a plastic bucket full of water on the beach. He also knows how to press a cell phone to his ear and pace in a tight circle, talking nonstop baby babble with all the earnestness of a corporate deal maker. I thank him for that. And who wouldn't be grateful for the great job he did of staying asleep while we sat in the courtyard outside his window to celebrate the last night of 2011 with beer and chips and shooting stars?

I am grateful to my son Jeff and to his wife, Monika, for buying a house on 1.25 acres outside West Palm Beach (so we could visit them in Florida instead of, say, Wisconsin) and for transforming their 1.25 acres into something like the little farmyards I saw in my grandparents' village in Hungary. (Monika is from Hungary too.) They've got flowers and vegetables, egg-laying chickens, brown ducks called Chocolate Runners, a hedgehog, three cats (one of whom lives with the chickens), and three dachshunds. The smallest of these is Peanut, a calm and matriarchal doxy, as they say, who oversees a varying population of cagelessly boarding dogs in small and medium sizes. There were seventeen Friends of Peanut on hand (and on laps and couches) for the holidays, and it was amazing to see how peacefully they ranged through several rooms and large parts of the yard (though not the chicken part). Equally amazing was the noise they made when a doorbell rang or a car pulled up.

I am grateful to my daughter Lauren for making sure we watched plenty of *Doctor Who* from Jeff's collection. I loved this not only because my children have been watching *Doctor Who* since they discovered him on IPTV twenty-five years ago, but also because it gave me a chance to get several good photos of my husband—an excellent traveler but not, as he would readily admit, a lover of dogs—sharing the couch with multiple Friends of Peanut.

And of course, we are all grateful to John not only for arranging our flights and accommodations and for driving the rental car, but for the sneeze that snuck up on him while he munched an after-dinner peppermint outside the Thai restaurant in Key Largo, sending hard white shards of candy flying out of his mouth. It was our daughter (thank you, Liz) who gasped and said, "Holy cow, I thought those were your *teeth*!"

I SEE LONDON, I SEE FRANCE

On Missing Our Date with the Ducs de Joyeuse

APRIL 2013

My husband and I recently received an invitation to a wedding in France, and, like the narrator in our favorite J. D. Salinger story, we thought we might just go, expenses be hanged. Among the benefits of attending — in addition to witnessing the vows of two Omaha friends who "met" at their fortieth high school reunion — were a ride on the speedy Train *à* Grande Vitesse from Paris to southern France and a weekend at the Château des Ducs de Joyeuse near the medieval town of Carcassonne, where the wedding would take place. The only downside was the fact that neither of us could get more than four days off from our respective jobs, which meant that we wouldn't be in France long enough to experience jet lag before we were back home again.

In the end, common sense prevailed. Our soon-to-be-newlywed friends were having a stateside reception in June, so it's not as though we wouldn't get a chance to celebrate with them. Sure, we'd miss out on the château, but I looked it up and actually the dukes' history was not all that joyous, despite their name. One Duc de Joyeuse — born in the château in 1560 — is famous for supervising the massacre of eight hundred Protestants at the battle of Saint-Éloi during the religious wars of the sixteenth century. In a subsequent battle, the Protestants did unto the duke as he had done unto them.

Still, on April 19, the day before the wedding, I wished that we were hurtling toward his château at 190 km per hour.

"Ah, well," my husband said. "C'est la vie."

He can talk. He was in Paris as recently as 2009. (See "Tales of a Happy Traveler.") Technically, I was in France in 2009 as well, with my sister, but only long enough to have a run-in with a French customs official at Charles de Gaulle airport en route to Italy, where I had a literary event to attend. He—the customs official—stopped my sister and demanded to search her carry-on bag for the bottle of water one of his colleagues had mistakenly "spotted" in Sandra's bag. It must have been "bottle of water!" that he kept saying over and over again.

"You don't speak English?" he cried when we failed to understand him. A vein on his forehead seemed about to burst.

I sometimes regret even now that I didn't come right out and ask the guy, "Qu'est-ce que vous cherchez, monsieur?" I had been, for a couple of school years, a high school French teacher, and while my vocabulary was limited, my pronunciation was not half bad. At the time, however, I had a feeling that if we followed up several minutes of not understanding his English by asking him what he was looking for in French, he would be so humiliated and angry that Sandra and I would miss our flight to Venice. And so we continued to fail to understand, as politely as we could. When the search of my sister's bag yielded no water bottle or anything like it, the Frenchman finally threw his hands up in disgust and stamped our passports, glad to be finished with these two Americans, who were obviously too stupid for words.

For me, his gesture—that backhand wave of disgust and dismissal—was like déjà vu all over again. It sent me straight back to 1974, when my husband and I were rather newly wed ourselves. We were spending the month in Paris, something that I felt was required of a freshly minted French teacher like myself. (A month was all that we could afford.) We registered for classes at the Alliance Française, where John learned to say "Ma voiture est verte" a statement that would, eventually, be true. The mottled blue Mustang we drove at the time would soon be replaced by a green VW beetle, followed in turn by a green Volvo wagon—as classic a sequence of voitures as any child of the sixties could ever hope to drive.

John also learned "C'est tout!"—an easy-to-pronounce ("Say two!") and useful phrase—when he was buying croissants one day, pointing at this one and that. When he paused, the lady asked, "C'est tout?" Ever obliging, John said, "Two!" although he really wanted four of them.

John made only limited progress en français. He spent most of our month in Paris in the Air Canada office. While I improved my intonation and updated my vocabulary, John tried to convince the airline agents that we had purchased two round trips from Chicago to Paris, even if our many-paged flight coupon booklets did not, in fact, contain the tickets for our return flights. Somebody in Chicago had made a big mistake and, in an age before email, cell phones, and Skype, John spent many a morning-to-evening in Paris, sending something called Telex messages to Chicago.

In case you're thinking that not checking our tickets to make sure they would get us to Paris *and back* pretty much qualifies as too stupid for words, well, sure it does, but there's more.

One Saturday afternoon, when the Alliance Française and Air Canada were closed, John and I took the Metro to the eastern end of the line: Vincennes. A forest, a zoo, a château. Something to take our minds off the fact that we might be in Paris for longer than we'd thought. We strolled between the trees to the château and joined a group of people gathered around a well-dressed woman. Delighted to understand her crisply enunciated French, I passed along to John the fact that Vincennes was built for Louis XIV and abandoned upon completion of the grander château at Versailles. (It was at Versailles the previous week that John caught an alarming glimpse of himself in the Hall of Mirrors. It looked as if he'd been shot, but the spreading red stain on his light blue shirt came from a hidden string bag of raspberries he'd brought along for lunch.)

At least, at Vincennes, our clothes were clean. The group dispersed, leaving John and me with the well-dressed tour guide, who changed the subject from Vincennes to something that wasn't getting through to me. I can't help wondering what we looked like to her: a long-haired boy carrying lunch in a stained string bag and a girl in a cheap flowered skirt from the sidewalk sale on the Boulevard St. Michel. That woman didn't know who we were or where we were going, and neither did we. I think now that she was trying to be tactful, but I never did get what she was talking about, and she never did get her tip. Like the French customs official of the future, she finally gave up, threw her hands in the air, and walked away.

After a moment, I translated: "She thinks we're too stupid for words."

I wouldn't want you to think that was the only impression we left on the French back in 1974. One time, after a restaurant meal in Paris, I made a stop in the restroom and then followed John through a maze of tables on our way to the door. How surprised we were by the smiles and nods that greeted us—even a smattering of polite applause—from the diners we passed. Not until we were out on the sidewalk did John fall a few steps behind me and discover that the hem of my light and flowery new skirt was caught in the waistband of my underpants. Ooh la la.

IF IT'S TUESDAY, THIS MUST BE HONG KONG

JULY 2012

B y the time you read this, my husband and I will be back in Iowa, our two-week trip to China a thing of the past. Right now, however, while it's Monday evening back in Iowa, it's already Tuesday morning here in Hong Kong, and I'm writing to you from the future to report that we've been having a remarkable time.

Reading to prepare for the trip, I came across these sentences in *Invisible Cities* by Italo Calvino:

"You take delight not in a city's seven or seventy wonders, but in the answer it gives to a question of yours."
"Or the question it asks you, forcing you to answer. . . ."

As our flight cruised at thirty thousand feet above half-frozen oceans near the top of the world, I realized exactly what question I hoped this trip would answer for me, namely,

Why are we here?

On our way to China, I mean.

My decision to visit Hong Kong and Beijing is kind of inexplicable, even to myself. I am not what they call an inveterate traveler. The idea of taking a trip just for fun or to see the "seven or seventy wonders" of a place is, well, foreign to me. I tend to travel for a specific purpose. I've taken students to France, taught a writing course in Dublin, traveled with a human rights group to Guatemala, and read my work at a literature festival in Italy. Most often, though, I travel to visit family or friends, or to research a writing project, or both.

So why *were* we here? Was it to visit our friend Judy, who's teaching in Hong Kong this semester? Why wouldn't we just wait till she got back to Iowa City and walk over to her house? *A bit of Hong Kong in your next book?* my editor wondered. I was noncommittal, but the answer, I'm pretty sure, is no. Had we come this far to promote my current novel? Meeting with the Women in Publishing Society at the famous Hong Kong Foreign Correspondents' Club would be cool, but was it 7,789 miles' worth of cool?

And what about the side trip we had planned? Four days in Beijing, where (we were warned) you couldn't count on finding someone who speaks English. We ran into linguistic trouble right away. To find our hotel we'd been told to emerge from the subway station at Andingmen and walk south. But which way was south? Without a compass or a working cell phone, there was no way to tell at noon on an overcast day. Personally, I don't worry much about getting lost because I never know where I am anyway—this is one of the benefits of having no sense of direction—but I sure wished that my *Speak in a Week Chinese* CDs had taught me the word for "south."

Aided by pantomime and a series of genuinely helpful citizens, we finally found the Hutong Culture Inn, a three-story building deep in a warren of one-story row houses, originally built in the fifteenth century for Ming dynasty officials and subsequently subdivided, and divided again, and again. Our room on the second floor had a view of modern solar hot-water tanks installed on venerable tile roofs, many repaired with corrugated metal and plastic sheets held in place by bricks. We had breakfast in the bar on the third floor, where the Wi-Fi always worked and the walls and ceilings were decorated with vintage posters featuring Chairman Mao.

On the first night, John and I walked naïvely into a restaurant where every table had a big hole in the middle. This was for the hot pot of broth into which the diners plunged their choice of ingredients. Handwritten in English on the list of meats that our waiter scrounged up for us were bullfrog, fresh aorta, and, we thanked our lucky stars, sliced mutton. Noting our hesitation, the waiter cheerfully demonstrated how to mix it all in with spinach, sweet potatoes, and noodles, and how to ladle it out without getting scalded.

We saw that waiter in the neighborhood every day after that, usually on his bicycle, and every day he recognized us and said, "Hello!" We answered, "Ni hao!"

I had studied a little Mandarin Chinese, which I actually used, much to the amusement of the locals. When a guy tried to interest us in a bicycle-powered rickshaw ride, I meant to say, "Bu yao," meaning "I don't want it," which is Beijing-ese for "No thanks." What I said instead was "Ni yao," meaning "*You* want it!" This was true—he did want us to buy a ride—and it made him laugh. Another useful one-liner was "Wo bu ming bai!" ("I don't understand!"). I got a laugh every single time I used it, which makes you wonder, but hey—everybody likes a good laugh. Just doing my bit for US-China relations.

Three days before June 4, Tiananmen Square was full of Chinese tourists confronted only by the hawkers of hats and souvenirs. In the Forbidden City, we found the Hall of Great Literary Merit and took a picture of me there. We hired a guide and a driver—Kevin and Gao—to take us to the Great Wall. They had a little trouble finding it, actually, so we got an extra scenic tour that took us past familiar-looking farmland, a vacation spot called the Fishing Village of Contemplation, and a paintball place.

We returned to Hong Kong after our weekend on the mainland and haggled over shoes and shirts and key rings in various street markets. (I was advised to start by offering half the originally quoted price and pass the calculator back and forth until the merchant "gives in.") We rode a city bus up hairpin turns to "The Peak"—the highest point in Hong Kong—and sat up there until darkness fell and the amazing light show of the skyscrapers danced around the harbor below.

We stood in the peaceful garden of a Buddhist monastery in Kowloon and saw not only the vertical lines of high-rise housing and office buildings sprouting up beyond the teak roof of the monastery, but also the tree-covered mountains the city is built on and into. We crossed the bay on the ferry to Lantau Island, where we found scattered villages, stray cows, large gardens, and many more bicycles than cars. (Elsewhere on Lantau Island are the international airport and Disney World.) We took a bus to Tai O, where the old British police station has become a two-hundred-dollar-per-night boutique hotel. A very short walk away, working fishermen and their families still live in a hodgepodge of odd-lot houses, perched on bamboo stilts above the tide.

I'm still not sure if I was asking Hong Kong and Beijing *"Why are we here?"* or if they were asking me. Either way, I believe I know the answer, which is

See all of the above.

One more thing. In case you're planning a trip to almost anywhere any time soon, my husband—the happy traveler—has some free advice for you. In the subway, when you see those signs on the escalators that tell you to Hold the Handrail, obey them. If, while juggling your luggage, you lose your balance and fall, the grooves on the edges of the moving steps will make you look like you've been in a fight with a tiger. Guess how John knows.

CRITTERS

PHILOSOPHER CAT FOR SALE

The World According to Miz Franklin

JULY 2002

For a long time I swore I would *never* write about cats. People don't want to read about how your cat can balance on the tippy top of her scratching post and so on. They don't want to read anything that begins "You should see" or ends "It's so cute." I know the dangers of writing about cats. If you're T. S. Eliot, you can write about cats, sure. If you're not T. S. Eliot, if you're the resident director of a college dormitory that doesn't allow pets so you wait for cover of darkness to bring cat litter in from the car, people are going to think that you're just another crazy cat lady.

You don't need ten cats to be a crazy cat lady. If you own cats in more than one state, I believe you qualify automatically. That's why I need to get rid of—I mean, I need to find a home for—my Omaha cat, Miz Franklin. The theme here could be expressed in three little words: Cat for Sale. Or even two: Free Cat.

I would keep her for my very own, believe me, if I didn't already have *two* cats in Iowa City who are scared to death of Miz Franklin, although she probably weighs less than half of *one* of them. When I took her to Iowa for a visit, my cat Ralph (a handsome male the size of a small horse) stayed under the wing chair and growled for three days straight, even while he was eating, at which time the growl turned into a deeply resentful "nyum, nyum, nyum."

I'd be the first to admit that Miz Franklin is a bit of a biter. She never sinks her teeth in or does any real damage. It's just a quick nip that sometimes means *Buzz off!* but more often suggests *Let's play!* She sees your hand reaching down at the end of your long arm, your fingers wiggling in anticipation of stroking her silky fur, and the same neurons that fire when you dangle her stuffed Dalmatian-on-a-rope in front of her start firing away. Pull your hand back or stuff it in your pocket, and she thinks, hey, *Hide and seek!*

You should see her with that stuffed Dalmatian, by the way. She's a very acrobatic cat. She dives over the thing, comes up from underneath, all four paws gripping it, and does a somersault (sometimes two or three) with her legs wrapped around this dog that's bigger than she is. It's so cute.

Sorry.

Apparently, Miz Franklin suffers from a kind of feline dyslexia that leaves her unable to distinguish between the human hand and a cat toy. I'd hate to hold that against her, wouldn't you? Miz Franklin's early childhood was traumatic. She was found under a car in the parking lot of the Creighton House one night in December. Two student residents heard her crying in the small hours of the morning. It was cold and raining, but their windows were open anyway. It's hard to regulate the steam heat in our vintage residence hall, originally built to house young women who left the farm for work in the big city. Students come down to meetings in the winter dressed in shorts and tank tops or jackets and scarves, depending on whether the heat is on or off on their side of the building. As fate would have it, Bill and Richard were on the hot side of the building that night, so they heard that kitten crying out there.

She's got a voice on her, Miz Franklin. A friend told me that means she's part Siamese, although she's all black and golden-eyed. She doesn't "miaou," as *French for Cats* so aptly spells it. She makes one long, open "anhhhhh" sound after another, like a car alarm. "AAANHHH, ANHHHH, AAANHHH," she says whenever the refrigerator door opens, or you take a step toward the kitchen, or she's stuck in the closet, or she *wanhhhts* you to sit down so that she can curl up in the center of her universe, which you happen to perceive as your lap. She particularly enjoys the lap of a person sitting at a computer, I've found, and she's very polite with the claws, unless you want to get up.

Now that she's bigger, she no longer needs to sink her claws into your leg while she climbs it like a tree trunk. And she loves the scratching post I snuck into the building! Not just for sitting on top of but for scratching instead of the furniture. I have been told by many friends with cats that this is virtually unheard of and much to be prized.

But back to that fateful rainy December night. Unable to sleep—"AAANHHH! ANHHHH!"—her rescuers took a bedsheet out to the parking lot and scooped her out from under the car. They brought her upstairs, dried her off, and fed her tuna, and thought they'd go back to sleep with a cute little kitten curled up at the foot of Bill's bed. After a period of hissing and toe-biting, tiny little Franklin (that's what they named her, thinking she was a he) spent the rest of the night in a storage closet (that used to be a phone booth in the working women's residence days) out in the hall.

That's where we found her the next morning—"AAANH HHH! ANHHHHH!"—a tiny ball of black fluff who stopped crying the moment we opened the door. She looked out at us while making another noise that we later determined was the sound of a very tiny kitten hissing. She wouldn't come out of the closet until a young man named Brandon went down on his hands and knees in the hallway and meowed repeatedly. We thought he was crazy, until the kitten came out of the closet, rubbing herself against Brandon's front leg—er, arm—and obviously thinking, *Are you my mama?*

No wonder the poor cat's confused. Every time anyone approached Miz Franklin (which is what we called her after her first trip to the vet), she would hiss her little head off. If you picked her up (in one hand, easy), she would keep on hissing until you got her settled in your arms, at which point she'd snuggle up against you in obvious relief and contentment. When you put her down, she'd look up and hiss again. She simply did not recognize the Human Holding Her and the Human Towering over Her as the same set of data.

Who can say she's the one who's got it wrong anyway? When you stand up, where *does* your lap go? Every time Miz Franklin sees the Hand That Feeds Her as a cat toy, she raises once again the question of whether perception determines reality, usually answering it in the affirmative with her teeth. Not too shabby, for a cat. Philosophers have built whole careers on that question. I mean, if a tree falls in the forest and nobody hears it, who cares if it made a sound or not? But if a cat yowls in a parking lot and if that cat happens to be Miz Franklin, you can be sure that some-body's reality is about to change. Could be yours. Make me an offer.

SQUEAKY BITES THE DUST

Legacy of a Yorkshire Terrier

MARCH 2001

My cousin Velma is an impeccable housekeeper. (I don't really have a cousin named Velma, but discretion requires a name change here. You'll see why.) Every place Velma has ever lived—from her first tiny apartment on Kinnickinnic Avenue in Milwaukee (or some such location) to the beautiful new home she and her husband recently built in Fond du Lac (wink, wink), Wisconsin—has looked like something out of *Better Homes and Gardens*: not a couch pillow or magazine out of place. Toilet, tub, sink, and tile gleam like alabaster in the bathrooms. In the bedrooms (except for the tornado-struck one occupied by her daughter), the beds are always made, sheets pulled tight and wrinkle-free under a bedspread that reaches evenly to the polished floor (or vacuumed carpet) on all sides. If you're the kind of person who goes around running your white-gloved finger over baseboards and windowsills, your gloves would never go gray at Velma's. She keeps a clean house.

Perhaps you'll be surprised to learn that Velma is also a dog lover. Specifically, she loved Squeaky (not his real name), the little Yorkshire terrier who lived under her impeccable roof for more than a decade, doing his part by chasing the occasional dust bunny out from under the bed and into the maw of Velma's vacuum. "Squeaky was more like a person than a dog," Velma said to me last Christmas, getting a little misty more than a year after Squeaky died of old age and diabetes. In his declining years, Squeaky needed insulin shots on a regular basis. This, in turn, required monitoring his blood sugar with a daily urine test. When I asked Velma how cooperative Squeaky was about these procedures, she said he didn't seem to mind the shot, which he always stood still for, but that it was hard to catch him at just the right moment for the urine test.

Squeaky was an indoor dog. Oh, sure, he went outside to do his business, and while he was out there, he might worry a stick or chase a butterfly (at least in his more youthful days), but most of the time he spent in the house, curled up and napping on my cousin's bed or perched like a sentinel on the back of the couch, where he could growl out the front window at anything that moved, from birds and squirrels to leaves that dared to fall from the trees onto the neatly raked lawn. Squeaky's favorite spot—I'm sure it comes as no surprise—was in my cousin's lap. "Even now I can hardly sit in the living room and watch television without him," she told me. I know just what she means too. What I missed most in the first winter after our cat Pooger died was the warm weight of her in my lap. The bond between people and pets should not be underestimated.

It was during the last year of Squeaky's life, when his declining health was evident, that my cousin developed her rash: a persistent itching accompanied by red spots like hives on her thighs. At first she thought it was a heat rash or maybe a reaction to the new and more powerful laundry soap she'd been using. Velma always had sensitive skin; heat or stress or the wrong kind of lotion often left her with raised welts that itched like mosquito bites. In the past, Velma's hives had always vanished without professional treatment. Even when the cause remained mysterious, they seldom lasted for more than a day or two.

This time, though, the rash persisted. My cousin tried the usual remedies: cortisone cream and calamine lotion, cool baths and hot showers, ice packs, aloe (straight from the plant), and baby powder. Nothing seemed to help.

Meanwhile, poor Squeaky was having more and more problems of his own. He had taken to sleeping on my cousin's side of the bed, and in the morning my cousin would wake to the sound of Squeaky whining in dismay as he peered fearfully over the edge of the bed to the floor so far below. She would scoop him up and carry him like a football to the back door, where she deposited him on the grass outside, often just in time. When he was finished, he would lie in the grass and wait for her to retrieve him, both of them exhausted, Squeaky by all the whining and fidgeting and Velma by the early morning dash to the door — not to mention the restless nights of itching and scratching. Their relationship had gone beyond sympathetic to truly symbiotic, Velma said. "When I scratched, he scratched. When he felt bad, I felt bad. We were miserable together."

By then, Squeaky was making weekly trips to the vet, who adjusted his insulin dose and reassured Velma that the dog was doing as well as could be expected. It was July, the weather hot and humid, and my cousin suffered in the long pants she had to wear to hide the little red welts that now spread from upper thighs to her knees. In desperation, she made a doctor's appointment for herself too. Since she was certain that the doctor would scoff at her theory that the mysterious rash was somehow the result of poor Squeaky's troubles, she stuck to a simple recounting of symptoms and the measures she had taken, in vain, to alleviate them.

Imagine her surprise when the doctor took one look at the rash and said, "Any pets at home?"

"Why yes!" Velma said. She told him about poor Squeaky and asked, "Do you think there's a connection?"

"I'd say so," said the doctor. "These are flea bites."

Velma went home and bombed the house — not with explosives, of course, although she was tempted. Then she spent a week cleaning. Every surface got Lysoled, every sheet and towel and item of clothing went through the wash on HOT with extra detergent, causing the demise of more than one wool sweater. Squeaky got a flea bath that perked him up considerably, at least for a while, and a bed of his own in the kitchen, where he slept out his remaining nights in closer proximity to the back door.

DUCKLINGS ON DODGE AND OTHER RESCUES

T he front door burst open. "You've gotta see this!" my husband said.

We lived on South Dodge Street in Iowa City at the time, far from any substantial bodies of water, unless you count the inflatable wading pools that college students furnish with lawn chairs and cooler, often within viewing distance of a television on the porch. We weren't used to seeing twelve tiny ducklings bobbing and peeping on the sidewalk across the street, apparently motherless and heading for two lanes of one-way traffic.

"Stop them!" I cried to a pair of college students lounging in the nearest front yard.

They shooed the ducklings back from the curb, just as our neighbor's cat Ethel came around the corner of the house. Unable to believe her good fortune, she dropped into a stalking stance. I bounded across the street, shouting, "Shoo, Ethel!" The cat barely glanced at me. The ducklings bobbed and peeped, oblivious. The college students groaned. Desperate now, I did an end run around the ducklings and spit in Ethel's face: "Ffffft!"

That did it. Ethel fled, the ducklings scattered across the neighbor's yard, and with my husband posted at the curb to make sure they didn't cross the street in two and threes, I went to call for help.

Taped to the wall in our kitchen is an envelope scrawled with the phone numbers of people we can call to find out what to do if a feral cat has kittens in our garage or a nest of baby robins falls out of the forsythia—all those hopeful open beaks!—or a gaggle of ducklings tries to cross our busy street. These are people we know only by first name and animal specialty (noted in parentheses after each name). When I came out again with the pet carrier that Jean (BIRDS) had suggested for gathering up the ducklings, the mother duck had already returned to the scene, dragging one wing theatrically across the yard before she headed in the direction her ducklings had taken. By the time help arrived, mother and ducklings were gone, except for the two we discovered peeping mournfully in a deep window well. "Ah," said Jeremy (DUCKS), who, thank God, was equipped to care for a pair of half-day-old ducklings. "This is why the mother left the group," Jeremy said. "She was trying to retrieve these two. A mother won't leave anybody behind if she can help it."

Maybe that explains it. I'm a mother, after all. At our house, we're always trying to rescue somebody: baby squirrels fallen from a tree, a feral cat with six little mouths to feed, fuzzy yellow chicks the kids found under a bush on their newspaper route after Easter.

Most of our efforts have been futile. You can't save a field mouse your son snatched from the jaws of your cat by pouring no-sting Bactine on its wounds. And even if you follow the vet's instructions, mixing the formula from the pet store and feeding it to the baby squirrels with an eye dropper, they are probably going to die, one after the other, a fresh grief each morning—even the one who opened its eyes and clung to your son's finger while sucking eagerly on the dropper. *This one's going to make it!* we thought. But no. Another hopeless case (our specialty).

The trouble is you can't tell which cases are hopeless. A bird crashes into a second story window and spirals to the ground. Is the bird going to make it? Probably not. But how can you tell?

I didn't see it hit the window, but I heard the THUNK from the porch. Looking up from my book to the house next door, I saw a bird flapping its wings desperately but sinking, sinking, the way you feel in dreams when you're running but you can't get away. Down it fluttered out of sight. I went on reading for a while, but that bird kept pecking at the corners of my consciousness. It became "he," as in, if he was on the ground, the neighborhood cats would be after him soon.

I found him beside the neighbor's driveway—a lovely olive-gray and cream-colored bird with a long beak and a ring of bright red around his eye, one wing folded neatly, the other spread like a fan on the gravel. He was breathing hard. When he saw me, he tried to flap away, but by the time I got back to him with rescue gear—a big cardboard box, a pair of thick suede mittens, and my daughter Lauren—the bird didn't have the strength to protest. Lauren scooped him up in her mittened hands, his heart pounding so hard we could see it, and into the box he went. We put the box in the storage shed my husband has cleverly built of old windows and doors. The next time we checked, the bird had flapped out of the box and landed crookedly on a pile of wood in the corner of the shed, his head fallen to one side. He did not look good. "At least the cats won't get him," Lauren said.

We didn't know what kind of bird he was or what he could eat, so we spread the floor of the shed with an all-you-can-eat buffet: water, bread, bits of fruit, and, in case he was not a vegetarian, a saucer of beer mixed with sugar to attract bugs. The bird showed no interest in our smorgasbord. He stayed slumped in the same spot until darkness fell.

In the morning, coward that I am, I sent my husband down, expecting the worst. John came back upstairs in a moment. "You'd better come take a look at this bird," he said.

To peek into our storage shed from inside the house, all you have to do is pull aside the curtain on one dining room window. I reached for it, but John stopped me. "Look at that," he said, pointing at another window. A bird who looked just like our guest was perched in a tree outside.

"He got out?" I said, amazed but hopeful.

John shook his head. "I think it's the wife." He shrugged. "Or the husband." He turned back to the window between the dining room and the storage shed. "Look," he said.

I pulled back the curtain.

What did I see? Directly across from me, our bird was holding onto the center bar of a window inside the shed, spreading and flapping his olive-gray wings against the panes, tapping on the glass with his beak in the hope of getting outside. That bird looked like the Holy Spirit hovering there. He looked like the resurrection and the life.

The bird keeping watch in the tree flew off when we appeared outside. (*Out all night, hunh?* she or he was probably thinking. *And come home smelling like beer?*) Our guest soon found the door we had opened for him and flew to some underbrush, where he rested for a long time. From there he made a slow upward journey from fence to clothesline to walnut tree, higher and higher, until the next time I looked he was gone.

We learned later that our bird was a black-billed cuckoo. It may be only a coincidence, but a pair of them have settled in our yard this summer. We also have a catbird, who serenades us every evening, singing like crazy out there, hardly sounding like a bird at all, hooting and tooting up and down the scale like R2-D2, going whistle, tweet, kazoo, and hallelujah!

ON SQUIRRELS

A Not-So-Lyrical Essay

JUNE 2000

Y ou can learn a lot about people from what they think about squirrels. And vice versa.

My husband was in a band once with a guy who liked squirrels better than rabbits because squirrels are easier to shoot. They have a tendency to stand there looking at you. (*Got food?* they're probably thinking.)

Beatrix Potter, on the other hand, must have liked rabbits better than squirrels. Peter Rabbit loses only his clothes while fleeing from Old Mr. McGregor; Squirrel Nutkin has to leave half his bushy tail behind to escape from the Owl.

A squirrel with a full-length tail but very little fur elsewhere showed up on our front porch once, shivering and hungry, its bare skin pink and wrinkled. When it stood up to eat the crackers we tossed out, it looked like a little old man in need of a jacket. (That squirrel would have been very easy to shoot, had we been so inclined.)

National Book Award–winning author Ha Jin, a native of China, said that when he first came to the US, he knew that he was in a place of affluence because of the squirrels. There were so many everywhere, he said, and nobody was eating them. (Except, perhaps, the guy in the band with my husband.)

A friend of ours took his wife and kids along to a medical conference in New York City years ago. They felt sorry for the squirrels they saw scurrying around in Central Park. Apparently, the poor things had lost all the fur on their long, rat-like tails.

On the Creighton University campus in Omaha, we've got squirrels who go out of their way to block your path and make eye contact, hoping for a hand-out. They have gray fur mixed with red, giving them a fiery look. I've seen more than one college student back down from a pushy squirrel.

I used to live in the Creighton House, a three-story, turn-of-the-previous-century building, whose brick walls were easily scaled by squirrels. They liked to perch on the deep window ledges and peer inside to see if you had anything for them. When opportunity knocked, Creighton House squirrels answered. A hole in the corner of a window screen led one of the more enterprising to make a nest in the space between the inside glass and the screen. The student living on the other side of the window thought this was pretty cute. She put food out for the squirrel and took to leaving the window open. Sure enough, after some hesitation, the squirrel would dart inside to scoop up the goodies and dart back out again. One day, the student forgot to close her window when she left for class. She came back to find the squirrel sitting on her desk munching on a Milk Dud from a box it had obviously torn open. "Hey!" cried the student. The squirrel promptly dropped the Milk Dud in its little hands, seized the box instead, and dashed out the window.

Nobody tried to shoot it though.

Some squirrels are suicidal when it comes to traffic. They wait at the curb until a car is almost upon them, and then they dash across the street. Perhaps they're playing chicken. I hit one once, many years ago, when I was driving the children to school. We all inhaled sharply, and I swerved, nearly causing a head-on with the minivan in the oncoming lane. Hoping for the best, I looked in the rearview mirror, and when I saw that squirrel leaping into the air, I thought I'd missed it—until it dove back down head-first into the pavement. Some crazy pattern of damaged neurons was making the squirrel leap, arch, and dive, over and over, as if it were underwater instead of sailing through the unforgiving air.

That was my children's second lesson in squirrel mortality. In fall of 1984, when my son was nine and his sisters six and three, three baby squirrels fell from a tree in front of their friend Kiva's house. The children fixed up a box for the baby squirrels, and Kiva's mother called the animal shelter to find out how to feed them. Every four hours, you could walk down to Kiva's house and find the children sitting cross-legged on the porch with a few ounces of gray squirrel in one hand and an eye dropper in the other, their faces grave, concentrating, watching to see if the little squirrels were getting the formula down or letting it run out over the children's fingers.

Two of the squirrels died without ever opening their eyes, but the third one looked more promising. He sucked eagerly on the end of the dropper and soon came scrambling to find the hand that fed him. He even took an interest in the ball and stuffed animals the children put in the box to keep him company. We have a great photograph of that squirrel getting his eye-dropper supper from my nine-year-old son, the squirrel's little hands curled over Jeff's finger, Jeff's head bowed solicitously over the squirrel. By then, we had moved the box down to our front porch. School had started, and it had fallen to me, a graduate student at the time, to come home for the noon feeding. For the first three days of the semester, I walked home at noon, mixed up a bit of formula, removed the screen we kept on top of the box to fend off cats, and lifted the squirrel out of the box—where he might be snuggled up against the stuffed animal or standing in a corner looking at me—to feed him. On the fourth day, I found him curved over the top of the ball he liked to climb up on, as if he were going for a ride. I almost picked him up before I realized that he was dead.

Perhaps it really doesn't pay to care more about squirrels—or anything else—than God and Beatrix Potter do.

If you really want to know about squirrels, search the internet. You'll find websites that feature "Amazing Squirrel Stories," "The Nut Lady Homepage," and the "Grave of Shorty the Squirrel."

At roadsideamerica.com I learned about three different towns that pride themselves on their populations of white squirrels. In Olney, Illinois, for example, law officers wear a white squirrel shoulder patch on their uniforms. You can bet it's illegal to shoot a white squirrel in Olney. As a matter of fact, it's illegal to run one over. In Olney, white squirrels always have the right of way.

And if that's not weird enough for you, check out the Cress-Fitch-Lawrence-Sanfillippo Funeral Home in Madison, Wisconsin, where in the basement you'll find Sam Sanfillippo's "perky dead animal dioramas," featuring stuffed white squirrels riding motorcycles and playing basketball and the like. Sam doesn't preserve the squirrels himself; he has a taxidermist do it. Still, I can't help thinking that if somebody—a human, I mean—wanted to go out, say, sitting in an armchair or posed with a rifle and a string of bagged squirrels, instead of lying in a casket, Sam might be the man to see.

BIG IDEAS

DAVID THE DECONSTRUCTIONIST

Signs, Snorts, and Supercats

DECEMBER 2012

My grandson David is proving to be a chip off the old Baka, which is what he calls me. Only two years old, and already the boy can read. Show him "C-r-e-i-g-h-t-o-n" and without hesitation he will say "Supercats!"

Now I know that when *you* see "C-r-e-i-g-h-t-o-n," you probably think, hmm, isn't that a top-ranking regional comprehensive university in Omaha, Nebraska? How does the boy get "Supercats" from that? If he said, "SuperSquirrels," that would make some kind of sense, since the squirrels on campus are quite aggressive. I've seen students back away from a fat squirrel that's planted itself on the steps of the administration building, chattering threats and brandishing its tail like a battle standard.

I first discovered that C-r-e-i-g-h-t-o-n meant "Supercats" while David and I were sorting the cards in my purse. David loves cards: money cards (both credit and debit), copy cards, AAA cards, library cards, "soupy" cards (from Panera), and more. I noticed that whenever he pulled out a Creighton University business card, he said "Supercats," and put it in the appropriate pile. Not long after that, my (handsome and precocious) grandson was heard muttering "Supercats" from his car seat when the car was stopped at a traffic light. Up there next to the stoplight was a street sign that said "Ed Creighton Avenue."

It didn't take long to figure out why "Creighton" had come to signify "Supercats." When I take my laptop over to David's house to play, the first thing we do is Google our favorite funny cat video on YouTube. (You know, there's the cat on the treadmill, the cat in the bathtub, the cat jumping out at a bear or eating with a fork or riding around and around on a phonograph turntable or, David's favorite, the cat disappearing into a quart-sized jar.) We start by clicking on the ball with the fox curled around it, and what pops up? My faculty homepage, C-r-e-i-g-h-t-o-n logo at the top. Mystery solved.

Some readers—while amused by David's powers of observation and overall cuteness—might say that the child simply doesn't know what "Creighton" *really* means, but, thanks to the work of French Deconstructionist Jacques Derrida, literary scholars know that what we are witnessing here is something called "the free play of signifiers." Excusez-moi? But of course you have heard of Jacques Derrida? And his Deconstructionist theory? Mais non?

Allow me to explain. First of all, "deconstruction" is not to be confused with "de-struction," as in, my father claiming years ago that he could put a solid block of stainless steel in the middle of the room and we kids would find a way to "destroy" it. Nor should we confuse it with the kind of interior demolition we had to perform on our 1856 vintage house in Iowa City, when we first bought it: tearing out lath and plaster and pulling up floorboards with a giant crowbar.

Deconstruction à la Derrida is less physical but more profound. What it destroys is the connection between words and what they signify.

Not making sense yet? That's kind of the point. Because there is no necessary connection between words and the world, none of us can be sure that we're making the kind of sense we think we're making.

Derrida doesn't get all the credit, or blame, for plunging us into a world where meaning is flexible, to say the least. It all began with a Swiss linguist named Ferdinand de Saussure. He's the one who changed words into *signs*. Apparently, until he came along in the late 1800s, everyone was pretty comfortable thinking of words as the names of things and actions and feelings, and so forth. People went around saying, "I'm going to sit under that big tree!" or, "Je vais m'asseoir sous ce grand arbre-là!" without giving a thought to the arbitrariness of the words they had just uttered. No one worried about the fact that the letters and sounds that make up the word "tree"—like those that make up "arbre" in French or "arbor" in Latin—have no necessary connection to the leafless maple outside my living room window, nor to the tree around the corner that's still decked out magnificently in red.

This fact did worry Saussure, or at least struck him as profoundly important. So important, that he came up with another word for "word." Each "word," he said, was a "sign" composed of two parts: the sounds or letters we can hear or see (which he called the "signifier") and the concept that the sounds or letters call to mind (the "signified"). Saussure even came up with a diagram of the sign to express the relationship between the signifier and the signified in, for example, the sign we know as "tree." In Saussure's diagram, the signifier (tree) appears below a line with the signified (a picture of a tree) above it.

We could draw this same diagram with "Creighton" (the signifier) below the line and the "Supercats" video (the signified) playing its Van Halen soundtrack above it. For that matter, we could put "Snort" (which is what David calls any large piece of construction equipment, having encountered a steam shovel named Snort in one of his favorite books) below the line and a power shovel or a crane above it. David loves nothing better than to stop and spell out the letters on a "R-O-A-D W-O-R-K A-H-E-A-D" sign and then spread his arms to embrace it all and announce with satisfaction: "Says 'Snort'"!

So what's the problem with this "free play of signifiers"? What's so de-constructive about it?

Here's the problem: If words—oops, sorry—if signifiers have no necessary connection to the real stuff they signify, it therefore follows, as "night" follows "day," that we human beings are totally and constitutionally out of touch with reality.

I guess that comes as a surprise to some people. (They must be people who have never watched TV in a swing state during a presidential campaign.) Derrida's ideas caused quite a stir. It bothered people to think that words, whether they are arranged to form poems or novels or the Congressional Record, have no connection to reality. Wouldn't that mean that our lives really *are* "full of sound and fury, signifying nothing"?

Truth is, I don't usually worry about that sort of thing. However, some kind of cosmic error was made at the aforementioned top-ranking comprehensive university where I teach, an error that resulted in my being assigned to teach a course in literary theory this fall. As a fiction writer, I have very little acquaintance with the likes of Saussure and Derrida. I might never have understood "the free play of signifiers" if it weren't for David, Snorts, and Supercats.

The beauty of being two years old is that you've never heard of Saussure or Derrida or even Shakespeare, and your contact with reality has been direct and tactile for as long as you can remember. Words, like all the rest of the world, are your playground, your personal domain. David has been known to grab a B word like "boy" or "baby" right up off the page and place it in my hand, an invisible gift, as he declares, "B is for Baka!" I believe we all know what *that* signifies.

UNNATURAL SELECTION

Regrets of a Spider Killer

L ast night I killed a spider with my shoe. It was on the wall in the kitchen, right at eye level, a black spider with a body about the size of a worn-down pencil eraser. I saw it when I turned on the light and immediately went to get a shoe. When I came back, the spider was in the same spot, tapping a leg (I almost wrote *tapping his toe*) tentatively, experimentally, against the wall, testing out the features of the suddenly new environment awash in light, and then—darkness. The quick shadow of my shoe approaching, followed by oblivion.

Remorse struck me immediately.

If I had looked at that spider a moment longer, I wouldn't have been able to do it. If, for a moment longer, I had watched the way the jointed legs found their purchase on the vertical semi-gloss of the kitchen wall, the exploratory wave of delicate antennae, the experimental movement of just one of the eight legs; if I had thought for another instant about the silk that black bead of a belly could produce, the intricacy of the web that would not be woven now, the eons—if that's the right word—of natural selection and adaptation that resulted in this member of the order Araneae in the class Arachnida from the phylum Arthropoda appearing on a kitchen wall in the latter years of my own species' sojourn on the planet; if I had considered its perfection of design, its ancient genetic code, the ATP exchanged so busily in each of its cells; if I had allowed myself another moment to recognize the astonishing evolutionary accomplishment tapping its spidery toe at eye level on my kitchen wall, I would not have been able to reduce it to a bit of juicy protoplasm on the soul (that's what I typed! a Freudian slip?) of my shoe.

In retrospect, it seems so wrong: the way the body was working perfectly one minute—a miracle of complex organization functioning without a hitch—and suddenly it's shut down, defunct, destroyed. You can probably tell that I'm finding it harder and harder to kill anything, even a spider or an ant. It's not a matter of warm fuzzy feelings for my fellow creatures, not a case of ethical principles or religious convictions that give me pause. It just seems wrong to smash a marvelous mechanism that's in perfect working order.

Not that I don't have warm, fuzzy feelings for my fellow creatures. When my cat Ralph died—after fifteen years of serving me as friend and "mews" (get it? he was my *mews*?)—I mourned him deeply. I miss him still. I've been known to grieve over dead squirrels in the road. I go out of my way to feed birds and deer and raccoons and more in our backyard (everybody loves birdseed), and the neighborhood cats know where they can stop for a snack (no, not the birds) or a drink of water year-round.

Those who know me best might say that I have for my fellow creatures an overabundance of compassion, "that Ache of Imagination," as my favorite Nobel laureate and Lithuanian poet Czeslaw Milosz defines it in one of his poems.

I spend many hours a day feeling that ache of imagination. It's my job, as well as my natural inclination, to imagine my way into other consciousnesses. I don't even need an animate object, much less a fellow creature, to make up a heart-wrenching scenario. Give me half a minute, and I can turn, say, a French fry forgotten in the bottom of the bag into a lonely protagonist, longing for the company of his salty fellows, little knowing the gruesome fate that has befallen them.

Speaking of that gruesome fate, eating one of those marvelous mechanisms is a different story for me. I tell myself (rationalizing my own carnivorous tendencies) that when a bird *eats* a spider, the spider molecules are reorganized into bird molecules, rather than disorganized into a useless smear on the bottom of my shoe.

It's different, too, when the bodily mechanism is breaking down gradually, naturally. As the priest cheerfully reminded us at my mother's funeral: "Guess what, people? We're all going to die." Even then, the moment when the machinery stops is striking, in and of itself. In a story called "Leaving Maverly," when a woman dies after years in a coma, Alice Munro describes the moment this way: "The emptiness in place of her was astounding. . . . She had existed and now she did not."

Here, the "emptiness" refers to the absence of the *person* animating the machinery of the body, but change "she" to "it," and the second sentence applies to the spider on my wall: it had existed —and now it did not. I don't have to think about *Charlotte's Web* or any other kind of personification. It's the senseless loss of a brilliantly organized piece of work that should have stopped me.

And usually, it does. I keep a clear plastic cup and an index card on the table next to the back door. When a moth or a lightning bug or even a fat blue fly follows one of us inside, I wait until it lights on the window, trying to get out, and then I put my catch-and-release insect removal kit into action. That's how reluctant I usually am to be a disorganizing principle.

There are exceptions to my reluctance. I'll slap a mosquito, of course, and centipedes—even the little ones—give me the willies. My husband says that any 150-year-old house is likely to have its share. I squash them with no hesitation, knowing how fast they move and how large and prehistoric-monster-like they can become and that they sting when they're cornered. (Ask my cat.) When I'm working at the table in our dining room and I happen to look up in time to see and *hear* something fall from the ceiling in the corner (not overhead, thank God) with a soft but distinct "thunk," you can bet I'm not going to let it take off running on its one hundred legs (if that's how few they really have) across the hardwood floor.

Oh yes, I know that centipedes are a marvel of genetic and mechanical complexity, too. I know their species has been around longer than mine and that they'll probably outlast us, provided we don't ruin the planet so thoroughly that nobody does. Still, when it comes to centipedes on the ceiling, I confess my willingness to add to the arsenal of Tennyson's "Nature, red in tooth and claw," my size nine women's shoe.

AGAINST MULTITASKING

Why a Day's Work Is Never Done

JUNE 2002

I'm glad to see that the experts have finally caught up with my mother's way of thinking when it comes to multitasking. A recent article from CNN.com wears the banner headline, "Study: Multitasking Is Counterproductive," with a subhead that warns, "Your Boss May Not Like This One." The study reports that people who compose memos, send email, and, say, answer phones all at the same time lose efficiency every time they switch from one task to another. "Not being able to concentrate for . . . tens of minutes at a time" may be "costing a company as much as 20 to 40 percent" in efficiency lost, the researchers say. "Time cost," they call it.

I say, surprise, surprise.

My mother knew the drawbacks of multitasking before the word existed. Back in the sixties, my summer job was sitting on the porch steps and watching my little brother play in the yard. Every day, I would try to sneak a book out there with me. My mother always snatched it, saying that I couldn't keep an eye on Ricky if my eyes were on the book. "You can't pay attention to two things at once!" is how she put it. She may have been right, but those were some long summer afternoons.

Multitasking is a computer term. It refers to the capability of operating systems to open more than one window—to do more than one task—at a time. I say, good for computers. Like it or not, we humans have only one window on the world open at any one time.

You can probably tell by now that I do not believe in multitasking. I don't even know if it requires a hyphen. (Nor do I care.) When I see the word, I picture someone on a unicycle juggling knives or flaming torches while playing the harmonica. Impressive but silly. Multitaskers are always riding for a fall.

This puts me (and Mom) at odds with prevailing practice in our you-can-do-it-all culture of cell phones, voice mail, and to-do lists of ever-increasing technological sophistication. Where once we jotted grocery lists and errands on the backs of envelopes, now we cram them onto palm-sized computers with memories large enough to accommodate Five-Year Plans for the Free World. Sad to say, while the microchip gets smaller and its storage capacity grows, the solar day remains locked at twenty-four hours and counting—a limitation that we are expected, these days, to ignore. I think we ignore it at our peril.

If idle hands are the devil's workshop, multitasking has to be his favorite occupational hazard.

State laws against using cell phones while driving officially acknowledge the dangers of multitasking. They're a start. Of course, surfing for a decent radio station, digging around for your sunglasses, and opening a can of Coke are also dangerous tasks while driving. My daughter reports having seen a woman on the freeway in St. Louis who was using a pair of scissors to trim her bangs in the rearview mirror while steering the car with her knee. Or what about the Chicago commuters I read about who prop a novel on the steering wheel in rush hour traffic?

Personally, I can't even sing and drive at the same time, except on cruise control. If I'm not punching the accelerator on the downbeat or speeding up with the tempo, I'm slowing down while I figure out a harmony or a murky stretch of lyrics. (Working out the French part in "Psycho Killer" once had me repeating "Qu'est-ce que c'est?" while poking along I-80 at forty-five miles per hour.)

Singing in the shower is a different story, though, in that it may prevent you from *thinking* in the shower, which is even more distracting than singing and thus more likely to make you forget if it was shampoo or conditioner that you just rinsed out of your hair.

Now I don't deny that there are some things you should be able to do at the same time, like walking and chewing gum or whistling while you work. And, admittedly, there are stories of inspiration sneaking up on geniuses while they were engaged in mundane tasks. One thinks of Archimedes shouting "Eureka!" while displacing water in the bathtub. And didn't Einstein come up with the theory of relativity while he was shaving or something? (We know that it was not while he was styling his hair.) I don't claim to be a genius, but I have been known to jot down the end of a story on a paper plate while stirring a pot of spaghetti.

The hazards of multitasking are not new. When I was growing up in Milwaukee, Judy Fecteau's mother used to set up her ironing board in the dining room, next to the window, within sight of her favorite soap operas on TV in the living room and her youngest daughter playing outside in the yard. Judy's little sister did survive to adulthood, but who knows how many times a steamy love scene (in those days, a kiss that lasted more than 1.7 seconds) on *As the World Turns* resulted in a scorched shirt or melted elastic waistband?

Mothers have always been the ultimate multitaskers, with or without cell phones and minivans. We could argue that multi-tasking is one of the many burdens that have held women back for centuries. It's pretty hard to write a symphony or a novel—or even assemble a stock portfolio or change the oil on the car—while you're cooking dinner, helping somebody with her homework, and feeding applesauce to the baby, all at the same time. Now squeeze in a full-time job on top of that, and you've got a lot of women multitasking their way through lives of not-so-quiet desperation.

It's not only the dangers of distraction that we should be worried about or the tasks done poorly because they're only half attended to. Multitasking has a deeper, more lasting and irrevocable effect. Multitasking robs us of mindfulness. It robs us of the quality of attention that makes us notice and remember things, the kind of attention that lets us get to know ourselves and the world around us. Instead of living in the moment, we're forced to live in four or five moments at once, which makes it impossible to savor any of them.

HERE COMES THE SUN!

Time for a Little Order and Beauty

The most remarkable sunrise I have ever seen came at me through a keyhole at the Western Paradise Motel in Ogallala, Nebraska. It was an amazing thing: a ray of reddish orange light shooting from the keyhole to shine like a spotlight on the wall behind the bed. My husband and I looked like bronze gods—or maybe boiled lobsters—in the glow. We thought we were about to be abducted by aliens.

I saw my second most amazing sunrise aboard the California Zephyr on the way to Sacramento, a trip we took to celebrate our twenty-fifth anniversary. We had dinner in the diner somewhere in Colorado, sharing a booth with Joe and Loretta, a couple we'd never met before, who happened to be celebrating their sixty-first. At one point, Joe passed his baked potato to my plate; he didn't eat potatoes. "Happy Anniversary," he said. It was also Loretta's eightieth birthday. She got the last piece of apple pie on the train.

Later, passing in predawn darkness through the moonscape that is Utah, we couldn't see a thing out the window of our sleeping compartment, just blackness. Then part of the blackness began to pale. It grew brighter and pinker, the sky separating itself from what we supposed was the land, when all at once, earth and sky—everything outside the window—went suddenly, shiningly pink. It was the Great Salt Lake out there, aflame with sunrise.

I've seen many of my favorite sunrises from a residence hall at Creighton University, where I teach. The windows of my little suite face east, and since Creighton House is on a hill, I have a fine view across downtown Omaha to Council Bluffs and the blue hills of western Iowa on the other side of the river.

Like a lot of writers, I jot things in notebooks. For me, the point is to gather in the richness, to get it all down before it slips away. In the past two years or so, I've jotted down an inordinate number of sunrises. I set my alarm to wake up for them. Sometimes I sit in a chair in the dark and wait for dawn. I don't know why I do this.

Some of the sunrises in my notebook are mere notations of date and time. Others are more elaborate:

Sept. 18. I'm sitting in a wooden chair directly in line with the sun, which takes only thirty seconds to clear the horizon. Through the window I see two suns out there, the real one that I can't look at and another phantom sun, reflected in the double-paned glass about two inches above and to the left of the real one. Of the two, the phantom sun is sharper and more convincing. Didn't Plato write about this?

Oct. 5. Sunrise at 7:28. Nothing fancy this morning. No heralding banners of pink cloud, rimmed in golden light. No banks of fog along the river bordered by blue trees. Just a tinge of orange above Council Bluffs, blue-black and twinkling.

Dec 15. At this time of year, in Omaha, the sun comes up on about 19th and Dodge. If the clouds are right, the whole horizon goes pink then tangerine and lilac, but the sweet spot, the red heart of it, is in the canyon between the (old) First National Bank and ConAgra.

Jan. 11. At 7:42, watching the sunrise from across the room, I'm stunned to see a great crane move slowly into the window frame, like a prehistoric insect or a bird. The crane, courtesy of Kiewit Construction, swings its long metal neck across the coral sky and leans toward First National, as if it were whispering secrets to a guy in an office on the sixth or seventh floor.

On one undated notebook page, I found a poem-like object. I bravely include it here:

> In August,
> the sun will rise again
> over the Civic Center,
> illuminating flat
> roofs and walls the way
> it lit the ballcourts
> of the Maya, blocks of stone
> trimmed in gold.
> On any given day, a Mayan
> woman might have sat
> on a flat stone and watched
> the stelae reaching up
> through lavender light,
> her day full of possible
> beauty.

The stelae, as you may know, are monoliths inscribed with Mayan glyphs that tell the stories of kings. I couldn't figure out how to get all that into the poem.

It really isn't like me to attempt a poem-like object. I usually stick to prose, mostly fiction at that. Writing fiction, I get to create characters and let them figure things out for me, characters like Arlo Johnson, who likes to watch the sunrise as much as I do. Arlo is nearly blind, due to macular degeneration, and he misses his dead wife, Emily, so much that he not only talks to her but catches glimpses of her from time to time in the blind spot in the center of his vision. Here's Arlo's (and Emily's) take on the subject:

> Watching the sunrise — slivers and slices of red melting to coral, purple fading to lilac and blue — gave Arlo a feeling of *Something's coming.* He liked the suspense, the undersides of clouds shot with light from below. Sometimes, just when

you thought it was all over, the clouds having paled to gray and spread out over the blue, covering the sun, something wonderful would happen: a hole would open in the gray and rays of the sun come shooting out of it.

Arlo felt closest to Emily at this time of day. She used to say that watching the sunrise was like looking into the past. It gave her a strange feeling, she said, to see the same magnificent display of color that the dinosaurs saw. Arlo wasn't sure that dinosaurs could see in color—some animals don't—but Emily said, *Hush, Arlo.* She said it was the same sunrise that Indian maidens looked at and Egyptian pharaohs and John the Baptist and her mother and father and her brother George. They were all dead now, but they had all watched the same sun rise. It's like we all watch it together, she said. It's where we all catch up with each other.

I think Emily has something there. We like to feel that we're all in the same boat—especially when we start to suspect the boat is sinking. Of course, the dinosaurs watched the same sun *set* as well. But a setting sun doesn't promise as much as a rising one. In the morning things seem possible. You don't yet know how little you'll get done that day.

It's all a matter of time. After you celebrate your twenty-fifth (or your sixty-first), those twilight years start looming larger on the horizon. Losses pile up higher than cumulus clouds. No wonder I look forward to the sunrise lately, even if it does occur at an ungodly hour. As my favorite Lithuanian-born poet Czeslaw Milosz says, "What is needed in misfortune is a little order and beauty." What could be more orderly and beautiful than the sun coming up again, on schedule, giving me the chance to seize another day?

ON LOCATION: IOWA

ONCE UPON LINN STREET

The Burg and I

JUNE 2012

My relationship with Iowa City's iconic Hamburg Inn No. 2 began before I ever set foot in the place. I was back in Milwaukee with the kids when my husband set out, a one-man scouting party, to find in Iowa City (1) a job; and (2) just the right counter-service restaurant to replace the breakfast-and-burger joint that had served as my office in Milwaukee. He was successful on both counts. I can still remember how happy he sounded when he called me to report that he'd spent a couple of precious dollars on a hamburger and coffee at this place called Hamburg Inn No. 2. It had a counter *and* booths, he said, and there were people reading and writing all over the place, especially at the counter. Also, the food was good, and the waitress had refilled his coffee cup before he even thought to ask.

All I had to report from Milwaukee was that my mother still couldn't believe we were taking her grandchildren to Idaho so that I could attend the Iowa Writers' Workshop.

It was 1982. In those days, the daytime waitresses tended to be women of a certain age. There was Micki, who was famous for remembering the "usual" of all her regulars even long after they'd finished school and left town; and Millie, who inspired so much loyalty and affection in two of her regulars—my friend Nancy Loeb and me—that when we heard she'd had a heart attack, we visited her in the ICU. We attempted to serve her a glass of ice water, but, lacking waitress skills of our own, we spilled it on her instead. The monitors went wild. Millie was okay but decided to pass on the glass of water.

195

The way I remember it, Dave and Mike Panther were always on hand. Mike was taller than his brother, broader of shoulder, louder of laugh; Dave was the quieter of the two, his inner clown waiting to emerge. Among our favorite waiters were Gary, your friendly lunchtime waiter, politico, and public access TV personality; Steve, greeter of US presidents past, future, and hopeful; and Paul, the one who changed his name to Gabriel after a while and always made himself into a very convincing waitress for Halloween.

Paul/Gabriel freaked my mother out one time, while she was visiting from Milwaukee. She and Lauren, who was four or five, were strolling on the pedestrian mall one day when a leather-jacketed man with multiple ear studs approached them and asked Lauren in his snickery voice what she was up to today. There was something about Paul—and I hope he would be pleased to hear me say it—that suggested both Ron Howard (as Opie on *The Andy Griffith Show*) and Truman Capote. My mother was alarmed by the leather, the hardware, and what she saw as the leer on his face.

"Don't worry, Grandma," Lauren reassured her. "Paul is one of my adult friends."

My children grew up with (or should I say, at) the Hamburg Inn. They were seven, four, and one-and-a-half when we came to Iowa City. The combined financial blow of starting graduate school, moving to another state, and quitting our jobs (!) in Milwaukee left us with little—actually, with no—money for fun or childcare. John found a job that allowed him to come home a little early on Tuesday afternoons so I could go to workshop, and I stayed home with the kids the rest of the week. We often roamed the streets, the kids and I, Lauren in the stroller and Elizabeth toddling along—Jeff, too, if school was out. Many were the times we wound up at the Burg, sharing a booth and an order of pancakes. Jeff won a potato clock during a promotion that involved weekly drawings for prizes. The more often you came in, the better your chances. It worked, too. The clock, I mean. The electricity came from two potatoes.

When Elizabeth was six and afraid to eat anything for fear of swallowing the baby tooth hanging by a thread in the front of her mouth, I took her to the Burg to entice her with a bowl of brown-sugared oatmeal. This was one of her favorite foods and, our waiter noted, one that she didn't need to chew. I will never forget the grateful way she looked up at us after her first mouthful, smiling bravely through her tears. The tooth was gone.

Years later, when Liz was in high school, she arranged to surprise her boyfriend with dinner at the Burg on Valentine's Day. I have a picture of them at the Presidential table, elegantly set with white tablecloth, candle, and a vase of fresh flowers, their waiter standing by in a secondhand tuxedo jacket and bow tie, a white towel folded over his arm.

Liz was not the only Stefaniak to host a special occasion at the Hamburg Inn. When my first book came out, Prairie Lights Bookstore owner Jim Harris came up with a great marketing idea. We'd have a drawing on the night I read at the bookstore, the prize a free breakfast with Jim Harris and the author at— you guessed it—Hamburg Inn No. 2. You might have had to buy a copy of *Self Storage and Other Stories* to enter, unless that was illegal in the state of Iowa, in which case, of course, no purchase was necessary.

But my literary relationship with the Burg goes back further than that. My very first author event in Iowa City—an after-hours reading with two poets—took place at the Hamburg Inn on a Thursday at 11:30 p.m., according to the flyer still hanging on the bulletin board in my husband's office thirty years later. The poets were Nancy Loeb of Tuscaloosa (she who helped me spill ice water on Millie the waitress in the ICU) and John Marshall of Seattle. While one of us used the seat of a centrally located booth for a stage, the other two served free coffee and apple pie at cost. Our publicist, fiction writer and fellow workshopper Brent

Spencer, designed the flyer in the manner of a menu, featuring dishes with punning names that honored writing and writers, especially those connected with the workshop. Faculty and visitors at the time included James Alan McPherson, Raymond Carver, Marvin Bell, Gerald Stern, Stanley Plumly, and James Galvin. Jack Leggett was director of the workshop then and David Hamilton editor of the *Iowa Review*. Breakfast offerings on our special menu included Egg McPherson along with Green Eggs and Hamilton. For dinner, there was Carvered Turkey, Leggett of Lamb, Stuffed Bell Pepper, and Variable Pig's Feet. Apple Sternover and Plumly Pudding rounded out the dessert menu. The house wine? Le Gal Vin.

My mother came to know Iowa City quite well over the years, but during her most recent visit—the first since she'd had a stroke that compromised her short-term memory—she had to be reminded frequently of where she was, namely, Iowa City, and why. When we asked her if she wanted to eat at the Burg, we expected the little frown, the puzzled pause. Instead, after barely a moment's thought, she said, "I'll have home fries." Her usual.

DRIVING IOWA

Where the Hills Are Alive

AUGUST 2001

I've enjoyed more than my share of scenery in the past year. Tall stuff, mostly. Last April, I was in Palm Springs, California, where the sky is so blue and the mountains so near that they look like paper cutouts against a blue screen. The palm trees, which are also quite tall, not only sway and rustle, they sparkle when the wind tosses them, as if the fronds were decked with tinsel.

In October, Colorado friends drove us through Rocky Mountain National Park to a point 12,080 feet above sea level. We were up so high that we could look *down* on snowy slopes and peaks. Last month, in Watkins Glen, New York, my husband and I walked up through a mile-and-a-half long gorge past waterfalls and whirlpools. (Is this, we wondered, where "gorgeous" comes from?)

But here's the weird part. After all that lofty scenery, my favorite landscape is in Iowa. Along I-80, no less.

Every other week from late August through mid-May, I make the four-hour drive from Omaha, where I teach at Creighton University, to Iowa City, where my husband and my cats reside, and back. People often commiserate with me about my commute, but the truth is that I like being in transit, neither here nor there. Except for occasional bouts of brushing up on "my Spanish" or "my Croatian" via *Teach Yourself* tapes, I do no multitasking on the drive. I drive, I think, I listen to music, and I enjoy the view. Western Iowa rolls away from I-80 in ridges and slopes and curves and undulations — a kind of preparation, when you're heading west, for the more dramatic Loess Hills that flank the Missouri.

I can't imagine what it must have been like—what kind of effort or machinery it took—to change the shape of these hillsides, crimping the earth into great ridges like the pinched edge of a pie-crust, leaving terraced fields that look to me like a pile of stacked-up muffin tops, or a full flounced skirt. Grass-covered berms hold the terraces in place. In the spring, the berms are bright green borders around black fields. In winter, the black earth is edged in white. If you are ever so lucky as to fly over western Iowa in clear weather, look down, and you'll see a landscape written in curves of earth like Mayan glyphs.

I think the winter landscape is best. If there's snow, the wind piles it in drifts along the highway and carves the drifts into caves and cliffs, the snow scalloped in little waves like a sandy river bottom. Unburdened by leaves, the trees are more expressive. Bare fields of black dirt look like dark chocolate brownies topped with powdered sugar, and no-till cornfields littered with broken stalks make me think of toasted coconut. I especially love fields dotted with round bales of hay, the kind that look like giant shredded wheat, frosted with snow.

I don't eat much before I make the drive; hunger helps me stay alert.

It's landscape as installation—a collaboration of nature and human effort. Who would have thought of putting a lone oak tree right *there*, where those two hills intersect, or cutting a jagged gouge through the green earth and making black trees elbow their way along the crooked path of that creek? Who thought to balance that red dump truck right on the top of a ridge, the payload raised at a pleasing angle, and to place behind it four round hay bales, evenly spaced, as if they'd just rolled off the truck and stopped there against the sky?

Sometimes in fall, when the sun is setting behind you, the dry cornstalks turn so yellow that where they meet blue sky, the colors blend, leaving each yellow hill outlined in shimmering green. Sometimes cows scatter themselves across a hillside; other times they line up in a row along the top of a rise and make a black and white fence against the horizon. Once, at the Henry Wallace rest stop near Adair, where the horizon appears to be within reach of your arm, a black cow walked across my field of vision with nothing but blue sky behind her, balancing on the line we used to draw when we were kids to separate the green-brown earth from the sky. Then she turned and stepped over the line, disappearing (head first, hips last) below the horizon, a cow setting like the sun.

I owe some of my appreciation for what I see through the windshield on my biweekly way across the state to my old friend Ellen Hickerson, who, come to think of it, grew up in western Iowa. Toward the end of her life, Ellen was nearly blind. I spent a lot of time describing things to her. This taught me to savor the details, to remember them so vividly that I could close my eyes and see the world the way she did. On a pair of hills near Avoca, Iowa, there's an oak grove where I'm sure the gods must stroll, only we drive by too fast to see them. Ellen would get the same kind of thrill I get out of that oak grove near Avoca; she would feel the presence of gods in the shade. For all I know, she may stroll among them now.

Another thing I like about the drive: those hours in the car are the only time I can really *listen* to music. I turn on the cruise control to avoid speeding up or slowing down with the tempo. Talking Heads, They Might Be Giants, Steely Dan, The Beatles, and a variety of string quartets and symphonies have all provided soundtracks for the *Here-I-Am-Driving-Down-I-80* movie that plays in my head.

Lately I've been listening again to *Appalachia Waltz*, an album that features Yo-Yo Ma, bassist Edgar Meyer, and Mark O'Connor, who was Johnny Cash's fiddle player, as co-conspirators — that's the only true word for what they do together — on a really indescribable collaboration that sounds, variously, like bluegrass, Irish tunes, old seafaring airs, and jazz. A few other instruments come in on some tracks — O'Connor on mandolin, Meyer on piano — but most of the music is nothing but one cello, one bass, and one violin doing things you wouldn't have thought possible.

My favorite is a tune called "Mama." At the start of it, Meyer's bass carries a growly melody so low to the ground it tickles your throat to hear it. If a bear could hum a tune, this is how he would sound.

Then Yo-Yo Ma comes in, and you forget that a cello is a musical instrument and not a living being with a heart and a soul and a passionate desire to do whatever Yo-Yo Ma requires of it. There are certain places in the music that make more than just your throat feel funny, pure but trembling sequences of notes where I know my friend Ellen, were she listening with me, would just have to scrunch her shoulders up and say, "Oh, my!"

IN MY OWN BACKYARD

All the Little Dinosaurs

Our yard is one-third vertical. The wooded bluff behind our house — from which the limestone foundation was quarried 160-plus years ago — stays brown long after daffodils have poked up elsewhere in the yard. From November through March and into April, the bluff is a climbable tangle of tree trunks and bare branches and logs and roots and deer paths and limestone outcroppings and dead leaves. At sunset, when the last beams of light shoot straight across our yard to the bluff, everything brown turns to gold — a reddish gold that gets redder as the shadows lengthen and the sun drops lower into the trees on the other side of the Iowa River across the street.

Then, one day in April, a green mist appears on the bluff. Buds on every kind of branch open into tiny leaves, on cue. By June, the vegetation is impenetrable — a lush three-story backdrop for fireflies.

The house itself stands in a smaller patch of yard, front and back, that makes a kind of plateau shored up by low walls and piles of stones, all of it bordered by trees. In summer, when everything is in full leaf, the patch of backyard that's closest to the house is like a room with living walls of greenery. Stepping out the kitchen door, you would never guess that Dubuque Street is out there on the other side of the thicket of trees and shrubs. You can see the Iowa River from our backyard, but only in the leafless seasons.

There's a break in the wall of trees on the north side of the plateau, where it slopes down at a modestly useful sledding angle to the lower part of the yard, which, for reasons I don't remember or never knew, we call the *sward*. (Sounds like "sword" the way it should be pronounced, "w" and all.) Some might call our sward a lawn, but given all the bluebells and clover and dandelions and vetch and jacks in their pulpits, "lawn" seems less than accurate. We do mow it, though, after the bluebells are done, with what we call the lawn mower.

We call the old stone steps that descend from plateau to sward "the garden steps," despite a distinct lack of "garden."

At its northern end, where our yard begins to narrow and grow muddier, the sward is blocked by the Great Barrier Tree, a fallen mulberry. Deer and squirrels and our one fat woodchuck have no trouble scampering over or under it. Only humans—including grandchildren—find it a formidable obstacle.

We are an official wildlife habitat certified by the National Wildlife Federation. Yes, I made a donation and sent for the sign that we've posted (without harming the tree) for all the raccoons, possums, foxes, cats, squirrels, deer, bees, butterflies, and birds—especially the birds—to see.

In the flower-pots-turned-birdfeeders that hang from shepherd's hooks not far from the kitchen door, we have at this very moment a sparrow (make that two sparrows—no, three), a chickadee, a tufted titmouse (come and gone and back again before I can get to the end of this sentence), and a lady cardinal who is turning around and around in the middle of the biggest hanging pot as if she's thinking *nest*.

To the birds who mate for life I sometimes want to say, "Don't do it!" I mean, it's worked out all right for my husband and me, but then our species is higher on the food chain than the birds. When I looked out the back door one morning in time to see a fox trotting away with something bright-red-feathered in its mouth, all I could think about was the lady cardinal sitting on eggs in a nest nearby, waiting for the breakfast that would never come. And few sights in the yard are sadder than an odd number of mourning doves pecking at the birdseed I've scattered under the cedar tree—especially when all but one of them fly away in pairs.

This morning, the long-haired semi-tamed calico that our neighbors call Peaches is sitting primly under a shelf of limestone halfway up the bluff, waiting for me to put cat food in the green dish at the bottom. I feed Peaches over there, at the edge of the sward, far from the flowerpots and the cedar tree, and she leaves the birds alone. It's a kind of extortion, I suppose.

I've never seen a cat carry off a bird in my yard, and I spend a lot of time here at the kitchen table near the windows, looking over the upper edge of my laptop screen at what's going on in the yard. As much as I love the birds, I couldn't begrudge the fox, who was feeding a pair of kits born recently in a hole on the far side of our driveway. And the hawk who swooped down on that unsuspecting mourning dove? Well, it's a *bird*-feeding station, isn't it? If I figured out a way to make it vegetarians only—no bugs, no grubs—about all I'd have left are the hummingbirds, who aren't strictly vegetarians either.

And speaking of DNA (weren't we?), doesn't the very idea that birds are descendants of the dinosaurs just thrill you to the core? We thought they were extinct—and here they are all around us!

I sit here in the kitchen and watch at least a dozen sparrows swoop as one from branches or roof to the birdseed under the cedar tree. Hopping over one another, splashing in the water dish, always moving, taking turns, sparrows are the hardest species to identify using the online lists for the Great Backyard Bird Count. Is that little guy an American Tree Sparrow (look for the black spot!) or a Song Sparrow or a Chipping Sparrow or a Field Sparrow?

They don't care what we call them, amateurs that we are when it comes to surviving world-changing disaster. They found a way to stick around, all these little dinosaurs, by becoming small and brown.

BOOKING IT

BOOKING IT, OR BON VOYAGE!

DECEMBER 2014

There is no Frigate like a Book
To take us Lands away,
Nor any Coursers like a Page
Of prancing Poetry—

Emily Dickinson wrote that.
You may be thinking that, sure, Emily Dickinson (1830–1886) thought there was no Frigate like a book, but she didn't know a thing about the internet, which can certainly take us to lands both near and far away, real and imagined. Reading as a way to escape must have been a real lifesaver during those long and snowy Massachusetts winters Dickinson had to get through, in the days before snowblowers and four-wheel drive. These days we've got our phones and tablets and computers, our PlayStation and X-Boxes to take us, virtually, worlds away.

Her poem continues, taking up the economic angle:

This Traverse may the poorest take
Without oppress of Toll—
How frugal is the Chariot
That bears a Human soul.

Others have expressed similar sentiments, though not, like Emily, in alternating four- and three-foot lines of iambic meter. There's a two-page ad, for example, in a recent *New Yorker* that quotes Belgian-born French playwright Francis de Croisset, who said, probably in French, "Reading is the journey of those who can not take the train."

And now we have something new. I read an article recently at technologyreview.com about "Oculus Rift," a virtual reality device that allows users to put on goggles that will pick up their every blink and expression and transfer them to their on-screen avatar, making the lips move and everything. The goggles, as I understand it, contain both the input devices (that sense your movements) and the output device (the 3-D screen on which you watch your avatar perform your every wink and blink and nod). The Oculus Rift was invented by a teenager (at the time) named Palmer Luckey, who may have been inspired by the goggles people put on to go barhopping in the Metaverse in Neal Stephenson's novel *Snow Crash*. *Snow Crash* was published in 1992, the year Palmer Luckey was born. Mark Zuckerberg owns the Oculus Rift company at the time of this writing.

By 2016, the engineers and programmers working on the goggles were going to solve what the article (entitled "The Quest to Put More Reality in Virtual Reality") called "the basic technical problem with virtual reality—how to fool the human visual system into perceiving virtual space as real."

Has anyone noticed that books don't have that problem?

Books use the human visual system (or the tactile, in the case of Braille, or the auditory, if the words are read aloud) to get directly *into* the human brain, where the reader's imagination *instantaneously* constructs the virtual space in which the story unfolds. There's no pixilation, no window-screen effect; there's just, say, an English tearoom on a rainy afternoon in 1944, where a bookish young American soldier is eager to hold up his end of the conversation with a girl named Esmé, in her tartan plaid dress, and her five-year-old brother, Charles, "whose cap she removed by lifting it off his head with two fingers, as if it were a laboratory specimen."

Perhaps you've already recognized what may be my all-time favorite short story, "For Esmé—with Love and Squalor," by J. D. Salinger. The American soldier, who narrates the story, first sees Esmé in a church, where he stops to watch a children's choir practice while taking a walk from camp into town. Consider the amount of computer code it would take to allow us to put on a pair of goggles and experience Esmé the way the narrator shows her to us:

> She was about thirteen, with straight ash-blond hair of earlobe length. . . . Her voice was distinctly separate from the other children's voices, and not just because she was seated nearest me. It had the best upper register, the sweetest sounding, the surest, and it automatically led the way. The young lady, however, seemed slightly bored with her own singing ability, or perhaps just with the time and place; twice, between verses, I saw her yawn. It was a ladylike yawn, a closed-mouth yawn, but you couldn't miss it; her nostril wings gave her away.

Or what if the point was to let you *be* Esmé in a scene like this? Could you put on the goggles and make your avatar yawn a closed-mouth, ladylike yawn? In the virtual reality of Oculus Rift, could your nostril wings give you away?

I guess we'll find out in 2016, when Oculus Rift and similar competing products are expected to be available, retailing "for only hundreds of dollars." Meanwhile, we've got at least one more winter to get through.

In the two-page ad I mentioned earlier, the quote from Monsieur Croisset (1877–1937) is invoked in support of the Kindle, something else that he and Dickinson would never have imagined. Personally, I'm a fan of books that smell and feel like books, with pages you turn, but ebooks and all the devices we use to read them have also solved the basic virtual reality problem. Books and ebooks both rely for their scene-to-reader interface on the same complex code — the same software, if you will — which is the ability of a literate human being to read.

I've got enough books stacked up to take me "Lands away"

through more than just one midwestern winter. Before long, I'll be going to Brooklyn (via *Motherless Brooklyn* by Jonathan Lethem), Havana (*King of Cuba* by Cristina García), the Indian Ocean (*Sea of Poppies* by Amitav Ghosh), and *October 1964* (by David Halberstam)—to name the first four frigates in my stack. I don't have to wait until 2016 to embark on these journeys either. No new software needs to be developed to enhance their virtual realities, no additional code is required. My brain is already programmed (thank you, A. E. Burdick Elementary School) to read them.

And so, obviously, is yours.

I'M NOBODY!

Who Are You?

APRIL 2002

I n airports especially, everyone looks like somebody you should
know.

Last month, in the United terminal at O'Hare, I was on
my way to AWP, which stands for Associated Writing Programs
and the big annual conference that all the writer-teacher types
attend as often as they can get their sponsoring institutions to
send them. Many of the familiar-looking people waiting with
me at Gate B3 for their flight to New Orleans might indeed have
been people I should know, whether from previous conferences
or the jacket photos on their books. I smiled and nodded at a few
familiar-looking faces, just in case. Some of them smiled back.

The "Do I look like you know me?" mood at the airport is a
preview of the conference itself, where you walk around for three
days feeling as if everyone is thinking that you're someone they've
heard of, perhaps grown older or paler than you look on your
book jacket. A second glance at your name tag usually reveals
that you're nobody very important after all, and their eyes skate
away from yours.

Still, there are many good moments at AWP. There are re-
unions, both planned and impromptu, with people you knew at
school but would like to see again. You might have dinner, or
roam the French Quarter, or even tour a bayou with folks you
haven't seen in years, people whose faces light up when they deci-
pher your nametag. You might even go to some readings and conference sessions — or be on a panel yourself. Afterward, someone

might come up and tell you how much they enjoyed your recent story in the *Podunk Review*. That's worth the airfare right there. If you're either bold or lucky, you get to chat with writers you've admired for years, whether they're famous or not.

In the hotel elevator, for example, I was lucky enough to meet Madeline DeFrees, a poet who must have been in her late seventies at the time. She was about five feet tall, sweet-looking. We had both gotten on a car that was going up, when in fact we wanted to go down, so we were taking a little ride together. After everyone else got off on the top floor, she reached for the nametag hanging on a cord around my neck and asked the question that everyone else was always thinking but afraid to ask.

"Are you somebody I should know?"

I flipped the nametag around (mine always had the blank side out) and said, like a dolt, "Oh, no. I'm nobody!" You can imagine how pleased I was when her face lit up anyway. "Stefaniak!" she said, squinting at my tag. Before I could even express my surprise —had she come across my book of stories? did she subscribe to the *Podunk Review*?—she remembered why my name rang a bell. She's doing research on Elvis Presley these days and had just been reading about his relationship with a secretary in Germany, a woman named Elizabeth (spelled with an "s," I learned later) Stefaniak.

I told DeFrees that I have a daughter named Elizabeth Stefaniak, and she has a grandmother named Elizabeth Stefaniak, but neither of them has ever met Elvis Presley. As far as I know.

Our elevator encounter aside, I have at least two personal reasons to be a Madeline DeFrees fan. She has a great locker room poem (as a swimmer, I spend a lot of time in locker rooms) and she used to be a nun—and writes about it. "In the locker room" begins like this:

> I surprise the women
> dressed in their bodies: in breasts,

knees, eyebrows, pubic
hair. Excitable children appear
to accept them.

Later, it continues,

> At sixty-five, I am less than
> a child, whose mother walked
> fearfully clothed, afraid of the water.
> My grip on the towel gives me away.

And it ends this way:

> Something has changed
> in the changing room where we step out of
> lingerie . . .
> and bring on the body in person.

And as a graduate of an all-girls high school run by nuns, how
could I fail to appreciate "In the middle of Priest Lake," where

> Sister Margaret Clare
> ships the oars and takes off her veil,
> her coif.

It turns out Sister Margaret's got a crew cut under there, in case
you were wondering. (And no, I myself am not a former nun.)

What I regret about my encounter with Madeline DeFrees is
my failure to follow up my doltish "I'm nobody!" by asking her
"Who are you?" Not because I couldn't read her nametag, but
because she is a poet and would, I felt sure, have responded, like
one of Pavlov's dogs to a bell, to the first lines of a famous Emily
Dickinson poem. If I had said,

> I'm Nobody! Who are you?
> Are you – Nobody – Too?

Madeline DeFrees would have said,

Then there's a pair of us!
Don't tell! they'd advertise – you know!

I would have come back with

How dreary – to be – Somebody!

Then she,

How public – like a Frog –

And I,

To tell one's name – the livelong June –

And then the two of us together,

To an admiring Bog!

I've seen this sort of thing happen, when poets and poetry lov-
ers get together. Marvin Bell was giving a talk at a conference in
Cedar Falls, when, to illustrate a point he was making, he started
reciting in an offhand way the Dickinson poem that begins like
this:

To make a prairie it takes a clover and one bee,
One clover, and a bee,
And revery.

When Marvin paused after the first "bee" and invited the audience to participate, someone immediately called out the second
line, then several voices shouted the third, and by the time we got
to the end, half the audience was reciting in unison:

The revery alone will do,
If bees are few.

Emily Dickinson is a favorite of mine for personal as well as po-
etical reasons. When I was sixteen, I took the highly experimental "creative writing" course first offered at Saint Mary's Academy

that year. (Madeline DeFrees also attended Saint Mary's Academy. Hers was in Portland, Oregon; mine was in Milwaukee, Wisconsin.) The creative writing teacher, Miss Mary Lou Jellen of the English department had a reputation as a hard driver. She was my first mentor and the finest teacher I've ever had, but at the time, she scared me to death. My little anorexic heart was pounding fearfully the day she took me aside and told me that if I kept at it, someday I could write poems like Emily Dickinson. As a high school sophomore, I was honored, of course. Much later, I realized just how fortunate it was that I did not ask Miss Jellen if Emily was a senior.

April is National Poetry Month. Read a poem. Write one. Emily would be pleased. For that matter, so would Miss Jellen.

GIANTS OR WINDMILLS?

They Might Be Both

MAY 2013

These days, it seems as though a giant has been handing out pinwheels along I-80.

If you're coming east from Omaha, as I do almost every week, you see the first ones peek up over the top of a hillside near Avoca. Then they drop out of sight again, not to reappear for several miles. Great white windmills are spinning in western Iowa. They're especially thick on the ground before and after exit 75, in the vicinity of Adair and Walnut: a forest of pinwheels by day, winking red eyes by night. I've read that MidAmerican Energy currently has more than a hundred wind turbines in Pottawattamie County alone. You can count a host of them from the highway.

In 2008 and 2009, when the wind turbines began to multiply, I was in the car on my weekly commute across Iowa listening to everyone's favorite sixteenth-century novel, *Don Quixote*, by Miguel de Cervantes—all forty and a half hours of it on thirty-five CDs, translated by Edith Grossman and ingeniously read by actor George Guidall. Guidall makes the Knight of the Sorrowful Countenance and his faithful squire Sancho so utterly real you expect to find them arguing in the backseat. At the beginning of chapter 8 (disc 2, track 11 on the CD), translated here by John Ormsby, they're arguing about windmills:

> "[L]ook there, friend Sancho Panza, where thirty or more monstrous giants present themselves, all of whom I mean to engage in battle and slay, and with whose spoils we shall

begin to make our fortunes; for this is righteous warfare, and it is God's good service to sweep so evil a breed from off the face of the earth."

"What giants?" said Sancho Panza.

"Those thou seest there," answered his master, "with the long arms, and some have them nearly two leagues long."

"Look, your worship," said Sancho; "what we see there are not giants but windmills, and what seem to be their arms are the sails that turned by the wind make the millstone go."

"It is easy to see," replied Don Quixote, "that thou art not used to this business of adventures; those are giants; and if thou art afraid, away with thee out of this and betake thyself to prayer while I engage them in fierce and unequal combat."

As we all know, the peerless Don Quixote, ignoring the protests and pleas of his squire, rides off on his bony steed to charge the nearest windmill. He gets his lance caught in one of the sails that Sancho warned him about and ends up somersaulting across the plain with his horse. The "undreamt-of adventure of the windmills" is probably Don Quixote's most famous moment, unless you count the part where he sings "The Impossible Dream," but that's not in the novel.

I owe my intimate acquaintance with *Don Quixote*, deliciously abbreviated DQ on my course syllabus, to seven years of teaching "World Literature I: The Beginnings to 1650" to groups of mostly reluctant college freshmen. I try to conduct the course (which bears a certain resemblance in pace and scope to the Mel Brooks film *History of the World, Part I*) like a Great Books club. Our chief goal is to read (as opposed to watching the video) and enjoy (as in, *Enjoy!*) a list of works that includes the usual— Shakespeare, *The Odyssey*, Dante's *Inferno*—but also the not so usual. Among them, in no particular order are *The Pillow Book* by Sei Shōnagon (a tenth-century Japanese work that is nothing like the movie); *The Chinese Book of Songs*; the poems of Sappho; and *The Conquest of Mexico* (from the Aztecs' point of view), which we read alongside the letters of Cortez and excerpts from the diary of Christopher Columbus, including this line, my personal favorite, noted by Mr. Columbus on Tuesday, 23 October 1492: "I want to leave today for the island of Cuba, which I believe to be Japan."

This is the benefit of a career in education, something it has in common with a life of writing: teachers, like writers, keep learning things. We see connections everywhere. If I hadn't been rereading Dante's *Inferno*, I might have overlooked the link I came across on a news website to a story revealing that archaeologists have recently confirmed the location of the gate to Hell. (FYI: It's in southwestern Turkey.) At last, we have a definitive answer to the question most frequently asked about Dante and Virgil, his guide to the multileveled underworld, namely, "Where in hell are they now?"

And what could be better than imagining Don Quixote's "fierce and unequal combat" with those windmills as I drive across Iowa watching wind turbines acquire their giant white arms?

While they were under construction, sharing the horizon with a variety of tall cranes used to lift them into place, I admit I didn't like them much. I worried about birds—real cranes, for example, flying into the blades, never reaching their springtime rendezvous on the Platte River in the middle of Nebraska. Standing still, the windmills looked ominous to me: a phalanx of three-armed, one-legged aliens marching across the countryside. *War of the Worlds*, they made me think.

But spinning! They're something else again. All of a sudden, you've got a giant pinwheel—and not just one, a row of them, several rows, a crowd of them marching north and south over rolling hills to either horizon. As Phoenix Jackson says about the pinwheel she's bringing to her grandson in "A Worn Path," my favorite Eudora Welty story, "He going to find it hard to believe there such a thing in the world."

I know they hum, though I can't hear them from the highway, and they do pose threats to wildlife, particularly the kind that flies. Like every human activity, from planting crops to driving across Iowa, the proliferation of great white wind turbines changes the environment in more ways than we know.

Still, seeing those windmills fills me with hope. If the Iowa landscape can sprout that many giant pinwheels, then it seems to me that all kinds of unlikely things could happen. We could be convinced to cut down on the number of cars in our driveways. We could be talked into walking. We could get in the habit of turning off the lights when we leave a room. Perhaps even I could learn to take the reusable bags into the store with me instead of remembering at the checkout that I've left them in the car or on the doorknob in the kitchen. In short, it seems to me that anything could happen, even the most undreamt-of adventure, the most impossible dreams.

POSTSCRIPT: As of December 2021, more than three thousand MidAmerican wind turbines are turning their giant arms in thirty-one counties across the state of Iowa.

HYSTERICAL PRESERVATION

HYSTERICAL PRESERVATION I

How to Bite Off More Than You
Knew You Could Chew

AUGUST 2013

S ummer 2004. For me, it was an exciting and anxious time.
Waiting for my first novel, *The Turk and My Mother*, to
come out in June, traveling around to readings when it did,
hoping for reviews and then being too scared to read them, teaching Iowa Summer Writing Festival classes, struggling always to
carve out enough time and concentration to keep *The Cailiffs of
Baghdad, Georgia* alive and in progress. There's nothing like a first
novel, I discovered, to get in the way of writing the second one.

You would think that I had enough to do, without taking an
interest in real estate, but the house for sale near the foot of the
bluff was on our way to almost everywhere. All summer we kept
driving past it. It was the house that Louis Englert, a brewer from
Belgium, built for his family over one hundred fifty years ago, the
one that had been a saloon, a stagecoach inn, and, it is widely
believed, a stop on the Underground Railroad. It was such an
interesting old house that my husband had gone through it back
in March 2004, not long after it came on the market. Intriguing
as it was, once he'd been inside, he could only shake his head.

"You'd have to tear out all the floors and half the plaster," he
said. (As it turned out, he had that backward: we tore out half the
floors and all the plaster.) "It reeks of cat."

We found out later that Aunt Dorothy (A.D. for short), the
last of her line to live in the house, had been an eccentric but
sociable soul. At least two generations of neighborhood children
from the houses up at the top of the bluff had counted on her

to let them climb down and play in her woods and in her cave. (Yes, there was a cave, the real estate agent told us, somewhere back there, hidden by vegetation.) A.D. would come out with cookies and lemonade for the kids. On the 4th of July, she'd invite friends to her screened-in porch to watch the fireworks launched from City Park, on the other side of Dubuque Street. At Christmas, she'd have an open house for all her neighbors and friends. They'd come, too, though their eyes would water and their clothes would get furry, for A.D.'s hospitality did not end with her human friends. In her later years she opened her home to an untold number of free-ranging cats.

I understand the impulse. My own house at the time was home to a pair of formerly feral cats born in our garage, and in the winter, my front porch was undoubtedly known on the neighborhood feline circuit as Stefaniak's Buffet. At A.D.'s place, however, things had gotten out of hand.

On top of the smell—or underneath it—there was the limestone foundation. It was crumbling in the walk-out part of the basement, also known as the saloon room, where someone had made the mistake in recent years of installing the kind of paneling that traps the moisture behind it. A few decades of walls sweating behind the paneling—while rain gutters more like hanging gardens than gutters let water run straight down the sides of the house—had resulted in piles of limestone rubble in the saloon room. When it was raining, a lovely little indoor waterfall cascaded into the room from one part of the wall.

So the place had problems. But it also had that screened-in porch with the view of the park and a bit of the Iowa River. (Little did we know how close the river would get to us as it returned to its old course, and then some, in the flood of 2008.) The house had real stone walkways, and two bay windows, and a lot of history, and a long wedge-shaped lot complete with a little ravine and a limestone bluff and woods and a cave.

We kept making appointments with the real estate agent to

go see it. Twice, to show we meant business, we met contractors out there—a concrete guy and a general contractor—and we got some estimates. We learned that it would cost about twice as much to fix this place (not counting the purchase price) than we had ever paid for a house in our lives. I told my husband that I rather enjoyed playing the part of a person who could afford to buy a place (i.e., to undertake a project) like this one. He said he was glad I was enjoying myself.

That summer, we walked out to the house at night, and in the morning, and in the afternoon, to see what it was like in different kinds of light.

Soon it was August. Time for John to start the semester at the University of Iowa and for me to start spending weekdays in Omaha, where I had been teaching for the past eight years at Creighton University. In Omaha, I was fighting for the time and space to work on the Cailiffs novel while I prepared and taught my classes and went to meetings and compiled the massive magnum opus they call a tenure application.

In Iowa City, John was still visiting the house. "I found the cave!" he said when he called me one night. "It's big! I can stand up in it!"

So in August we ran up our phone minutes discussing offers and counteroffers at all times of the day. The sellers believed that the historical value of the house made it worth a great deal more than we could possibly afford to pay for it, given the cost of making it fully habitable again. In the end, the condition of the place worked in our favor. A lot of potential buyers and history buffs looked at the place, but we were the only ones to make an offer. I guess everybody else was scared off by the eye-watering smell and the water feature in the basement. Although he proceeded boldly, even my husband admitted to feeling a *little* nervous at times about what we were daring to undertake.

Not me, though. Maybe it's a side effect of my endless struggle to be a writer, some kind of collateral courage I've developed in other areas, but taking on the renovation of a 150-year-old former saloon and stagecoach inn didn't scare me at all. From where I sat, saving that old house, as huge a project as it would be—worrying about it, spending every weekend helping John scrape and paint the exterior, prying up the hardwood floors, putting on our masks to tear out lath and smelly plaster, deciding what we could afford to do and what to give up and how to pay for it all—this looked to me like the easiest thing I'd do all day.

As my friend Judene's mother used to say whenever I said things like that—live and learn.

HYSTERICAL PRESERVATION II

Foundations 101 or Surprise, Surprise

SEPTEMBER 2013

Before we decided to buy the 150-year-old house we'd been looking at for months, before we knew anything about construction loans and the itemized estimates they require, I adopted a triage method of thinking about costs. My first question: What would it take to deal with the piles of limestone rubble in the walk-out part of the basement? From the comfort of our little house on Dodge Street in Iowa City, where we'd lived for twenty years, I made an appointment with a contractor — a concrete and foundations guy — recommended by the real estate agent (who was probably getting tired of meeting us at the house every other day). The concrete guy came out to have a look. He walked with us from the ground-level garage down three concrete steps into the basement.

There were three rooms down there, separated by limestone walls about twenty inches thick, each room a step or two lower than the preceding one. The first two were typical below-grade rooms, a little dungeon-like, but with taller ceilings than you'd expect in a house this old and those interesting "rubble construction" walls of irregular limestone. The concrete floor was clearly a newer development.

The third room, two steps lower than the middle one, was the walk-out, a twenty-by-twenty-foot room that had served as the saloon, we were told, back in the days when the house was a stagecoach inn. The saloon room had a nine-foot ceiling (a plus), two exterior walls of crumbling limestone half hidden by water-buckled sheets of paneling (not a plus), and one whole wall of casement windows and two doors (fifteen glass panes per door) that looked west across Ridge Road and Dubuque Street to Terrell Mill Park. A tiny corner of Iowa River could be glimpsed to the south.

Whether by nature or professional training, the contractor never so much as raised an eyebrow while he inspected the walls. He didn't even blink at what turned out to be a sizable hole worn clear through the two-foot-thick limestone in one corner (a water feature, we already knew, when it rained). His eventual verdict was that the saloon room's exterior walls—about one half of the whole foundation—would have to be "demo-ed out" and replaced with ten-inch concrete blocks. The remaining walls looked pretty solid, he thought (perhaps by comparison), at least from the inside. Additional costs included excavation, installation of drainage tile (which is actually plastic pipe), and backfilling the excavations with drainable gravel. He'd mail us a ballpark figure next week.

I was sitting on the front porch of our house on Dodge Street when the postman handed me the envelope, please.

According to the estimate, replacing not quite one-half of the foundation would cost more than the purchase price of our first house, a nice Milwaukee duplex we bought in the 1970s. The number produced a little bit of sticker shock in my husband, a lifelong do-it-yourselfer unaccustomed to paying for repairs and remodels. The general contractor's itemized cost sheet for everything *but* the foundation was still to come. That one added up to almost *three times* the cost of our first house in Milwaukee.

Emily Dickinson has written, "After great pain, a formal feeling comes." Somehow, having survived the shock of that estimate made us feel official, as if the die had been cast. Our summer's worth of dreaming firmed up into a formal offer to purchase.

We closed on the sale September 27. By the second week in October, the house was flanked by trenches one story deep and four feet wide. They ran the whole length of it, north side and south, from the end facing the street to the end nearest the bluff. Exposed now from the outside, the old limestone walls were all but indistinguishable from the earth. (Without the dirt behind it, the water feature hole was like a window, daylight shining through.) As the structural engineer from the city put it, shaking his head, "These walls have far exceeded their service life." The foundations guy needed to know what we wanted to do about them.

"Take 'em out!" John said. "All the way back!" And the replacement of not half, but the *whole* foundation was underway.

I've always admired John's email to our general contractor, calmly informing him of our decision to replace the whole foundation. The email ended, "We are going to look hard at all the cost sheets some more to see how we can afford it."

I was in Omaha, teaching, the week they dug the trenches, but my husband kept me informed with calls and emails reporting things like "They tore off the front porch today!"

That weekend, I got my chance to stand in the front-yard trench on the south side of the house and look *across* the wide-open basement to my husband standing in the backyard trench on the north side of the house, nothing but house-jack pillars and a Ditch Witch — a digging machine that looks like a snowmobile — at rest between us.

The equipment was a great source of joy for John: a front-end loader, a power shovel, the Ditch Witch (his favorite), the mini cement-mixer. All these toys in his yard! He ran around with a camera the day the footings were poured for the new walls. There were *ten* men working in the yard that day, all playing on his team.

John himself played a key role. Earlier that morning, two fellows had shown up in a special cement truck with a power pump to pour the fresh concrete into beautifully straight and regular footings lined up where the old limestone walls used to stand. From these footings, the new walls would rise, block by block, to meet the rest of the house, waiting—hovering—above.

The cement truck pulled up and stopped on Ridge Road below the walk-out, no doubt blocking both lanes. The men got out, shaking their heads.

"Hey!" John called happily to them. "This is the place!"

They looked less happy, peering up the impossible incline, frowning at the canyons on either side of the house.

"This truck's not *going* up this hill," the driver said. "I don't know *what* they were thinking. No *way*."

"Not here," John agreed with the cement truck man. "But if you back up and turn into the driveway—back there?—you can go around the other side of the house. That's how the power shovel got in."

The cement truck man looked greatly relieved. "I'm glad you were here," he said, "because, man, there is no *way* we can get this truck up in *here*. How *old* is this place, anyway? Do you know?"

Old enough to be a stop on the Underground Railroad, John could have said, citing multiple reports of bricked-up openings leading to underground tunnels and caves in the yard.

But that's a story for another day.

HYSTERICAL PRESERVATION III

Interior Demolition

Mysteries abound in an old house like ours—particularly in a house rumored to have been a stop on the Underground Railroad. The Pownalls, who bought the house in 1928, reported finding a round stone, three feet in diameter, beneath the old wooden floor in a basement room. They told Iowa City historian Irving Weber that the stone covered what seemed to be a bricked-in tunnel under the house. The daughter of George and Maude Ball, who had sold the house to the Pownalls, remembered that "her father bricked up a tunnel that ran to a cave in the yard."

The cave in the yard had already thrilled my husband, you may recall. He still likes to lead visitors into it after dark and make them turn off their flashlights. It's clearly man-made: a ten by fifteen-foot room with an arched stone entry and a stone ceiling that curves down from a height of six feet in the middle to touch the floor on each side. The ruins of other stonework suggest that the cave might have been inside another building at one time. There's no sign of a tunnel into or near the cave—which is a lucky break for our visitors.

We couldn't look for the Pownalls's basement tunnel without breaking up the more recent concrete floor, but lo and behold, when the water-buckled paneling came down in the saloon room, there was in one corner a roundish opening in the limestone wall, filled in with bricks and concrete blocks.

"Looks like a door, doesn't it?" my husband said to the foundations guy.

The next day, while digging trenches to expose the foundation, the excavator uncovered, on the dirt side of that "door" in the basement wall, not a tunnel but a little room the size of a closet with red brick walls and a curved brick ceiling. A little room *under* the backyard with a doorway into the basement. Was it a root cellar? A beer cooler? (Englert was a brewer, after all.) Or was it a hiding place?

All very intriguing, but with the house up on jacks and the limestone foundation ready to fall "like a stack of books" (as one workman described it) and a six-month construction loan deadline looming and a whole house to take apart and put back together by then, we had no time to find out.

As a matter of fact, we were in a bit of a crisis. We had already handed over the purchase price of our former stagecoach inn and closed on the loan that would allow us, as Ezra Pound might say, to "make it new," when we learned that the single biggest-ticket item of the renovation had suddenly doubled: not half but the whole foundation had to go. In hopes of paying for it, we sat down and did a line-item veto on the project cost sheet, saving five thousand dollars here and seven thousand there. Our very understanding general contractor received more than one email like this one: After further inspection, deliberation, and calculation, we have decided that we will scrape and paint the house ourselves. All items related to replacing the siding will have to be deleted.

That saved us about twenty thousand dollars right there. Of course, it also meant that we would have to scrape and paint the house ourselves. And that was, frankly, the least of it.

The number of tasks that moved to the Stefaniaks' to-do list continued to grow and eventually included such things as framing in a bathroom, building beadboard closets in the bedrooms, sanding and finishing all the upstairs floors, and putting up the ceiling (tin tiles over drywall) in the saloon room downstairs; but all of these seem almost incidental compared to the first and biggest of our jobs—the tear-out.

It all had to go: the lath and plaster on every wall and every ceiling; bushels of squirrel nesting materials behind the walls (including bits of canceled checks and junk mail and nuts and two squirrel skeletons and one cat skull); all the woodwork (some to label for reuse, some to discard); a lot of old pipes; all the hardwood floors in the living room, front hall, and dining room; and everything in the kitchen—except for one historic wall cabinet.

Interior demolition. As our daughter Lauren put it, "There is no experience quite like your parents taking you into a room, handing you a crowbar, a dust mask, and safety goggles, and telling you, 'Just tear all this out.'"

These were the months when friends who came by to check our progress grew pale behind the masks we gave them at the door. (Inspectors from the bank looked worried too.)

We couldn't have done it on our own. Much of the time, when John told the contractor he had "help coming in from out of town," he meant me, but often our daughter Liz and future son-in-law Van would make the four-hour drive from Omaha with me. Lauren, our youngest, had picked just the right year to spend in Iowa City before she started graduate school. Our only hired hand was Ed, a former graduate student of mine, then a starving artist.

While the contractor's men worked on the foundation in the ditches alongside the house, we were inside piling broken lath and chunks of plaster into wheelbarrows that we rolled out a door and across a wooden bridge that spanned the ditch, over the heads of the foundation guys, and into the backyard. From there, we rolled up another ramp and emptied our loads into the dumpster, raising clouds of dust.

Prying up oak floorboards with a five-foot long Burke bar became one of my specialties. Another was extracting nineteenth-century flat-sided nails from all the woodwork we had carefully removed. I even worked an extraction scene into my novel, complete with the screech of reluctant nails giving way. (See page 90 of *The Cailiffs of Baghdad, Georgia*.)

Long after the new foundation was in place, we were still shoveling and hauling. It took us from September 27 to December 19 to get the old stuff out and the furnace on and the plumbers and electricians in. When the drywallers finished their work—taping and sanding on stilts!—we walked around the house in awe. After months of nothing but studs between the rooms, suddenly this looked like the inside of a house again. We were practically finished! Nothing to do but prime and paint the whole interior, put in cabinets and fixtures in a couple of bathrooms and the kitchen, finish the saloon room, do the floors upstairs, paint the historic metal roof, and (this was the clincher) put back all the woodwork—"every stick of wood," my husband said—that we had taken down: doorframes, window trim, and, after the floors went in, about a thousand miles of baseboard that had to be replaced for olfactory reasons. Lauren got to be very handy with a miter saw. This, together with her math skills, made her an ace at fitting odd angles in the window bays.

Plus, we had another mystery to solve. Liz was tearing out plaster in a bedroom upstairs when she noticed something red on the boards behind the studs. Then something black and something yellow. "Come look at this!" she called. She had exposed a long stretch of exterior wall on which someone had pasted a long strip of paper a long time ago, inviting us to come and see "The Greatest Show on Earth!"

HYSTERICAL PRESERVATION IV

Boards and Circuses

NOVEMBER 2013

I t's hard to imagine how excited people around here must have been the first time the circus came to Iowa City. It was on a Monday in September, two days after the show in Des Moines, one day before Davenport. There must have been a crowd to meet the circus train, which was fifty railroad cars long, an 1877 circus route book tells us. One hundred and seventeen horses! Twenty-five animal cages holding lions and tigers and at least one bear, plus a live hippopotamus! Whether P. T. Barnum called it his Great Traveling Exposition and World's Fair or simply the Greatest Show on Earth, people must have lined up to watch the elephants and camels being led from the train. How many of them had ever seen an elephant or a camel before the circus came to town?

They must have been at least as astonished as we were when, in the course of tearing out the walls of an upstairs bedroom in our former stagecoach inn, our daughter Liz spied the first signs of what lay hidden behind the plaster. There were words on the boards back there, she said—and pictures! "Come and see!" she called to me in the next bedroom. I squeezed through a pair of hand-hewn studs and soon we were wielding our crowbars side by side, exclaiming to one another in mask-muffled voices as chunks of plaster fell, revealing pictures of—what? Was that a foot? And perhaps—a barrel? A pair of bare legs? In dainty boots? A horse's—tail? The dust rose and then settled around us. Finally, we stepped back and took in what we had uncovered.

The entire wall of the bedroom—an exterior wall made up of twelve-inch boards formerly covered by lath and plaster—was papered with circus posters.

They were in strips and pieces as wide as the boards they were pasted to, some words and images right side up, others upside down, but there was no mistaking them. Along with "The Greatest Show on Earth" and "Well worth going 100 miles to see," we had uncovered the chests and pounding hooves of horses whose upper halves, we cleverly theorized, were on boards that faced the outside, under the clapboard siding. Balancing acts and trapeze artists appeared here and there, in whole and in part and in various sizes. A woman in buttoned boots and a scandalously short skirt seemed to be lifting a barrel with her teeth. (This, we learned later, was "Millie DeGranville, the Woman with the Iron Jaw.") In another picture, on another board, she lay back with an anvil resting on her midsection while a shirtless man with a handlebar mustache hoisted a sledgehammer over the anvil, as if in midstrike. (Apparently, she had an Iron Stomach too.)

In other rooms, we found lettering that spelled out things like "P. T. Barnum," "Music Chariot," and "Iowa City," "Saturday," "Sept 8." A poster fragment in the bathroom promised "A Stupendous Bear" and "The Only Living Hippopotamus" in America, billed as a "Behemoth" "worth $20,000." In a corner of the master-bedroom-to-be, a pair of bare-breasted ladies posed demurely.

It was recycling, mid-nineteenth-century style: a roadside barn or mill dismantled, the boards once papered to advertise the circus put into service a second time.

My first impulse was to call all our friends to come and see—maybe the local paper and the historical society too. Circus posters brought to light after a hundred and fifty years seemed like both news and history. Then I remembered the deadline on our construction loan. We had a lot more interior to demolish and haul away before our contractor could move on to plumbing, wiring, insulation, walls, and so on. We called just a few friends and took plenty of pictures. Then we covered all the poster-bearing walls with heavy-duty craft paper, ready for the insulation man.

But we weren't through with those circus posters, or maybe they weren't through with us. In the summer of 2007, while I was looking into camels for *The Cailiffs* novel, we made a research stop at the Circus World Museum in Baraboo, Wisconsin. The very nice people at the library there were fascinated by our story of recycled boards and circus posters. They helped us hunt through files and catalogs for a poster that matched the pieces we had discovered in our house. No luck there, but when it came to finding out what year P. T. Barnum played in Iowa City on the "Saturday, Sept 8," our poster fragments advertised, all we had to do was look at a few early route books, the librarian said. Circuses kept daily journals that listed not only dates and places but how many miles were traveled on a given day, what the weather was like, and whether any "mishaps"—like the "Season ended by fire at Hippotheatron on December 24, 1872"—occurred.

We told the librarian that we would need to see route books from the mid-1850s. Our house was a former stagecoach inn and, it was widely believed, a stop on the Underground Railroad. In fact, I had recently read in *Nineteenth Century Home Architecture of Iowa City* by Margaret N. Keyes that abolitionist John Brown might have once stopped at the inn. Local historian Irving Weber reported a construction date of 1857.

Suddenly, the librarian looked doubtful. "Well," he said, "I can see a few problems there."

The first problem was that P. T. Barnum didn't take his circus on the road until 1871. The second problem was that P. T. Barnum didn't even have a circus in 1857. The librarian believed that Barnum was still firmly based in New York City at that time, exhibiting Fiji mermaids and the like at his American Museum.

We turned to the route books. In 1871, P. T. Barnum and his

newly traveling circus hadn't ventured any farther west than western New York state. In 1872, emboldened perhaps by the successes of the previous season, the circus had crossed the mighty Mississippi and played dozens of towns in Missouri and Iowa and even Kansas. The first P. T. Barnum show in Iowa City was on Monday, September 9, 1872. The next one was in August 1875. We finally found our "Saturday, Sept 8" in the route book for 1877. (The weather was fair that day — a nice break, I'm sure, after rain in Des Moines.) We couldn't help noticing that 1877 was more than a decade after the Civil War. A little too late for the Underground Railroad. Maybe too late for a stagecoach stop.

We left the Circus World Museum feeling bereft. If part of the house was made of boards advertising a show in 1877, did that mean all the long-held lore about our former stagecoach inn was, in a word, incorrect? Were we all living proof that, as P. T. Barnum himself reportedly said, "There's a sucker born every minute"?

Find out in "Hysterical Preservation V."

HYSTERICAL PRESERVATION V

Which Does Not Contradict What Is Known

DECEMBER 2013

I guess nine years is as long as you can expect a feverishly scraped, hand-brushed exterior paint job on 150-year-old wooden siding to last. By the summer of 2013, nine years after we purchased our pre–Civil War stagecoach inn, we knew we had to do something. We decided to replace the old siding with "cement board"—long pre-primed boards that look like wooden clapboard made new. When we took the old siding off the back of the house, we weren't exactly surprised to find the sheathing underneath haphazardly plastered with strips of circus posters— P. T. Barnum here and Millie DeGranville, the Lady with the Iron Jaw there, plus elephants, horses, the hippopotamus.

The house looked even more like a colorful picture puzzle on the outside than it had from the inside nine years before, when, in the course of tearing out interior walls, we first discovered circus posters on the boards beneath the lath and plaster. We were thrilled, until we learned that P. T. Barnum's circus hadn't come to Iowa City until the 1870s. How could a house built in 1857 be made of recycled boards that advertised P. T. Barnum's circus? And if the house wasn't built until 1877 (the date of the posters we found), then how could it have been a stop on the Underground Railroad? How could John Brown the firebrand abolitionist have visited the saloon that our walk-out basement used to be?

Afraid that our discovery debunked a lot of long-believed lore, we kept our circus posters to ourselves back in 2004. Now here they were again.

We needed a bold new theory, one that accommodated both the Underground Railroad and the 1877 posters.

I found one on a visit to Milwaukee. An architectural historian who was showing me around an old house there pointed out that the high-ceilinged basement in which we were standing was, at first, the whole house. The two-story frame structure above us was added later. Back home in Iowa City, I looked again at our pictures of the excavation in 2004, when the old foundation had to be replaced, and saw the different colored layers of dirt that made us think, back then, that the limestone walls of the walk-out had been more exposed and less like a "basement" when the house was first built. I remembered that in Margaret Keyes's notes for her book, *Nineteenth Century Home Architecture of Iowa City*, our house was described by someone as "a three-story house, the first story of stone."

It seemed clear to me that the ground floor of our house — the saloon level — is the pre–Civil War part. The rest of it was built on top of that "first story of stone" sometime after 1877. When I looked for evidence to support my theory, an Englert family photograph taken on the porch of the house circa 1890 led me to a family history by one of Englert's descendants. There I learned that Louis Englert's young friend and fellow business-man Jacob Hotz (1853–1916) was, among other things, a building contractor. Being a fiction writer myself and knowing that Hotz would eventually marry Englert's daughter, Frances (1859–1934), I imagined a story that, in the immortal words of fiction writer Donald Barthelme, "does not contradict what is known."

Louis Englert would have been in his late sixties when young Jacob Hotz first suggested the idea. Why not construct a two-story house on top of the low stone building tucked into a hillside just north of town, where Englert — a brewer, remember — had been operating a stagecoach inn and saloon for twenty years already? By 1878, stagecoach travel was limited to nearby towns, but Walter Terrell's mill across the road still brought in plenty of business. There was no reason the Englerts couldn't keep the saloon open downstairs while they enjoyed two whole new floors of living space above it.

I don't know how many of their twelve children were still with them then, but I can't imagine that Englert's wife, Clara, would have objected to living in a two-story house instead of upstairs from the brewery on Market Street.

Jacob Hotz, the young builder, would have done a fine job for his future father-in-law. He would have placed the exterior boards diagonally at the corners to keep the frame house so straight and true that a buyer in 2004 might open the double-hung windows with a single finger. He might have cut the lumber in his own sawmill, except for the twelve-inch boards recycled from somebody's roadside barn—the same barn whose owner had gotten himself free tickets to the circus in 1877 by allowing the display of great colorful posters days before the circus train arrived with its fifty cars full of wonders.

And perhaps young Frances Englert made her first impression on her future husband Jacob Hotz while construction was underway. I can see her in the yard with her younger brother Frank (thirteen at the time) and sister Clara (eleven), the three of them laughing with delight at the exterior wall going up like a great picture puzzle: part of a horse here and an acrobat there and the "Hippopotamus, Behemoth of Holy Writ," and elephants cavorting around the name of "P. T. Barnum."

At this point in the story, you may wonder if there is evidence that any part of the house is as old as it's supposed to be. Yes, there is. If Jacob Hotz had built the limestone foundation in 1877 or so, he would have used cement mortar to help keep those eighteen- to twenty-four-inch-thick walls from falling over like a stack of books. The blocks and chunks of limestone in the walls that stand between our saloon room and the basement rooms behind it are stuck together (or held apart) with older, crumblier limestone mortar, supporting an earlier construction date—say,

1856 or '57. Also, there's a great limestone chimney down there (in the very room where a round hole in the floor might have led to a tunnel, and so forth). Above the saloon level, the "newer" chimneys were built of red brick.

Allow me one more semi-historical reenactment.

When Louis and Clara Englert woke up one morning after another night of heavy rain in the spring of 1881 and betook themselves to the side porch of their new home overlooking the Iowa River, they must have been surprised. Until that spring, the river flowed straight to the bluff below the house. From there, it took a right turn to the south toward Iowa City, running alongside the dirt road that later became Dubuque Street. Across the road, the water flowed noisily over Walter Terrell's dam, turning the waterwheel in his mill.

What lay before the Englerts this morning looked less like a river and more like a lake with an island in the middle. The Flood of 1881 had washed out Terrell's dam and created a wide shallow backwater that turned out to be perfect for cutting blocks of ice. Louis Englert's son John would operate Englert's Ice Company in Iowa City for decades to come. In summer, the slow-moving backwater offered new recreational possibilities. Before and after the turn of the twentieth century, you could rent a canoe at Fitzgerald's Boathouse and paddle out to The Island for a picnic or even a lover's tryst. When the Pownalls bought the house in 1928, they could still watch canoeists and picnickers from the same porch that gave the Englerts their view. The backwater was landfilled to make Terrell Mill Park by 1940, but even today, we can see from our porch the ghost of The Island—or maybe its skeleton—in a slightly sunken stand of mature trees, a ring of them, leaning away from each other as if over the water, in the park across the street.

MY BRAIN EVENT

MY BRAIN EVENT I

Let's Make a Deal!

I was in Milwaukee, at my sister's house, for my mother's eighty-fourth birthday party. We were about to do the cake and candles part. It was 2009. I was standing at the sink in the bathroom, washing my hands, looking at my face in the mirror, when I felt a tap in the back of my head. It was so distinct that I turned around to see if I had backed into something, like a pull cord hanging from a light fixture. There was nothing hanging behind me. The tap had been inside my head, and as I turned around to face the mirror again, a sheet of pain (maybe a six or seven on a scale of ten) began to spread from the spot where I'd felt the tap. The pain moved in three directions—out to both sides and forward. When it reached my eyebrows, it moved up behind my forehead, so that within a few seconds I was wearing a kind of helmet of pain. Nothing excruciating but enough to make my sister ask me, after we sang *Happy Birthday* but before we cut the cake, if something was wrong. I looked a little funny to her.

Before I knew it, I was riding shotgun with my sister at the wheel and my mother in the back seat. I held a bag of frozen peas to the back of my head while we discussed where to take me—the nearest Urgent Care? a hospital emergency room? It was about 7:30 on a Saturday night. We decided on the ER at St. Luke's, the hospital where my siblings and I were born and where my mother used to work. She still volunteered there once a week, pushing people around in wheelchairs. It was also the hospital where pretty much everyone I knew who was now dead had died, but that didn't occur to me at the time.

The only really bad moment in the whole emergency portion of my health care experience was the CT scan. This is a procedure by which your much abated headache (so much abated, in fact, that I was wondering what the heck I was doing here) is transformed into the "worst headache of your life," as described in all the literature.

"This is making my head hurt much *much* more!" I hollered to the technician who had tilted my head back at an excruciating angle and then scuttled guiltily into a little control booth in the corner. "It's hurting more now than it ever has in my whole *life*," I elaborated. A tinny loud-speakerish voice told me to "Hold on."

"I think I might be ready to throw up now!" I warned. (In the ER, they kept asking me if I needed to.) No sign from behind the window in the little room.

"*Remember Rule #1,*" I exhorted, adding, in case the technician was dozing that morning in Medical Ethics 101: "*Do No Harm!*"

Afterward, I was provided with a no-splash-back "comfort" bag for the short ride back to the ER cubicle. (I'm happy to report that I didn't need to use it.) Untilted, my head felt better already, and things were looking up as far as I was concerned, when here comes the ER doc. She folded her arms on the side rail of the bed and announced, in a voice of portent, that the CT scan was positive.

I said, "Positive for what?"

Blood in the brain, she said. A very small amount, she added, but I could tell how impressed I should be. Suddenly I remembered the way they'd sent us right in, ahead of everyone else in the emergency waiting room, when I strolled up to the counter and mentioned the tap I'd felt in the back of my head.

I said, "You mean I'm going to be admitted?" She said, "*Oh yeah.*"

Having delivered the bad news, the ER doc got out of the way, and a young woman with a kindly face and colorful scrubs rolled a portable desk-like thing close to the bed. She handed me a pen.

Here were the papers that would admit me as a patient to the Neurosurgical ICU, where they could poke, prick, and prod me at will and even drill a hole in my head, if needed. They'd already photocopied my insurance card, so money would be no object.

Possible outcomes presented themselves to me like the doors on "Let's Make a Deal." Pen in hand, I asked myself which would I rather be:

SUDDENLY DEAD? (That was Door #1)
A PERMANENT VEGETABLE? (Door #2)
or (Door #3) ADMITTED TO THE
  NEUROSURGICAL ICU?

It was, no pun intended, a no-brainer: NONE OF THE ABOVE. Going home seemed like the obvious choice to me, especially now that my headache was almost gone. The trouble was that everyone else in the room (including my mother and my sister) wanted me to stay here and let them load me up with powerful stroke-and-seizure-preventing drugs, while we waited to see if there was a crucial line leaking—and perhaps about to blow—in my brain. To them, going home looked like choosing, or at the very least risking, Door #1.

Now for a startling confession. They say there are no atheists in a foxhole, but I can tell you that the brain works in mysterious ways, especially when it's under attack. Here I was in a foxhole, so to speak, surprised to be hoping that the atheists, wherever one might find them, were right! After all, if there was no God, then I would simply blink out like a candle, right? As a person who had recently finished reading Dante's *Inferno* with my World Literature class and being possessed of a vivid imagination myself, I couldn't help thinking there were fates far worse than going out like a candle. (Apologies to Dante, by the way; I don't think this is the effect he was going for when he described all those sinners getting poked, pricked, prodded, frozen, hooked, and cooked in excruciatingly gruesome detail. And some of them were down there for nothing worse than lending money at interest! I mean, where would they be now?)

I was all but ready to put down that pen and take my chances on blinking out like a candle, unmolested by medical science, when something else occurred to me. About a month ago, my agent had called with an offer from a publisher for the novel I'd been working on for the past six years. We'd accepted the offer, but I had not yet received the contract. Given the timing, I thought, it might be in our mailbox back in Iowa City right now, waiting for my signature to close the deal. What if the publishers were already regretting the deal (I fantasized darkly) and wishing they could take it back? There was no way they were getting out of publishing the book that I had spent the last six years of my life writing just because I died before I could sign the contract.

I signed the papers for Door #3.

To be continued!

MY BRAIN EVENT II

Dire Straits (and Rolling Stones)

APRIL 2012

When we last saw our heroine, I was checking into the Neurosurgical ICU at a hospital in Milwaukee, determined to retain my faculties long enough to sign the contract for my new novel.

It was like being on the space shuttle in there—no difference between night and day, lots of blinking lights and things that beep. I couldn't just float off wherever I wanted to go because I was hooked up to things.

Perhaps you know, dear reader, exactly what *total bed rest* means. I did not. For the next few days, whenever I needed to sneak out of bed to use the space-age, full-sized, stainless-steel toilet hidden in one of the cabinets against the wall, all my cords and lines had to go with me, carefully draped to avoid setting off any disconnection alarms that would call the nurse.

My nurse the first evening was Josh, a very kind and good-looking thirty-something, a former college wrestler, he said. (Picture a cross between Brad Pitt and the young John Travolta.) He had two little boys with names like Winslow and Homer or possibly Fenimore and Cooper. All the nurses in the Neurosurgical ICU were young and good-looking. Gazing out the glass wall toward the nurses' station was like watching an episode of *Scrubs*.

My mother and my sister spent that first night with me, my sister in the recliner, which she repeatedly offered to my mother, and my mother, whose birthday it was, in a straight-backed chair against the wall. (*Happy birthday to you!*) I don't remember which one of us said it—powerful stroke-and-seizure-preventing drugs were coursing through my brain already, although I don't recall feeling woozy, just nicely relaxed—but someone remarked, "We'd better call John."

My husband is a musician. At approximately 9:30 p.m. on Saturday, October 24, 2009, he was playing a wedding with a band called Twist and Shout at the Moose Lodge in Iowa City, 250 miles from Milwaukee.

"He won't hear it," I warned as my sister dug my cell phone out of my purse. I guessed they were doing the dollar dance at the wedding about now.

Storing numbers in my brain instead of programming them into my phone has long been part of my personal campaign against memory loss. I wondered if I was about to lose a lot of valuable data. So far I'd been able to tell anyone who asked me that I was in the Neurosurgical ICU at St. Luke's Hospital and that Barack Obama was President. I had no trouble pushing the right buttons to call John, although something started beeping on the IV tree when I lifted the phone to my ear.

We'd decided that I would be the one to leave the message; the news would be less alarming, coming from me. I couldn't avoid "hospital" and "brain" but ended cheerily with "I feel fine" and "Call me." Nurse Josh came in to see what set off the IV alarm.

An hour passed. My sister called my daughter Liz, who lives in Omaha. Liz consulted her "EXTRA SPECIAL Twist and Shout FULL ACCESS BACKSTAGE PASS"—a laminated card handily strung on a necklace of gold plastic beads—to find phone numbers for the rest of the band. When they finally took a break at the Moose Lodge, TJ, the drummer, gave his cell phone a quizzical look. Kevin, the guitar player, did the same.

It was almost eleven when John called. I told him I felt fine and asked, "Did my contract come?"

"Contract?" he said.

"For my novel! Was it in the mail today?"

"The mail?" he replied.

"Don't forget to bring it when you come!"

Five hours later, John poked his head into the gap in the curtained wall beyond the foot of my extremely comfortable air-cushioned bed. (More than once it has occurred to me that it's too bad most people in the Neurosurgical ICU are in no condition to appreciate the beds.) I could only imagine how I looked to him—better, I think, than his worst fears. His face downshifted quickly from stoic good cheer to something more genuine. We kissed, of course. He said, "Well, this is a heck of a deal."

I shrugged, setting off another alarm.

The contract was not in the mail. For all I knew, people were sitting around their editorial offices in New York, regretting their offer and hoping I'd been run over by a bus before I could sign anything.

In the morning, I had my first MRI. It was a noisy business —a lot of clanging and banging at close quarters and unpredictable intervals, now a ringing "A" note near my right ear, then a lower tone growling on my left. It was like Philip Glass performed on jackhammer and electric drill.

For the cerebral angiogram scheduled a little later in the day, I was nervous, I admit. The thought of a very thin tube traveling up through my femoral artery and around my heart to my brain was not a relaxing thought. Happily, the lovely sedative they give you right before they start actually puts you in the mood for such a thing. I was told that I wouldn't remember the procedure, but I recall not only the Dire Straits medley playing on the radio (followed by the Stones) but also the cold hands and the warm blankets and the road map of my brain's arteries projected on a screen for all to see.

Like the MRI, the angiogram was inconclusive. It just so happened that my "small stable bleed" had occurred in the vicinity of my rather "bulbous basilar summit." (You'll have to trust me on that.) The bulbousness could be the normal nonthreatening shape of my arteries, or it could be trouble. Although I was impressing everyone with my total absence of stroke symptoms—even my headache was minor—I'd have to stick around another whole week to find out what was up.

By now I'd been away from email long enough that people were looking for me. Concerned about my blood pressure, my husband almost didn't tell me when my editor's area code showed up on my phone. Her message—"Trying to get in touch. Call me!"—was cheerful with a hint of alarm. She didn't *sound* like someone calling to say she was sorry but they weren't going to publish my novel after all; too bad I hadn't signed the contract already!

I did my best to keep from kinking up the IV line while holding the phone to my ear. Indeed, Alane was *delighted* to hear from me. She had already edited the manuscript, she said, and wanted to send it along for my approval.

Did I mean to mislead her when I told her I was unable to respond to her emails due to being "at the hospital" in Milwaukee, where my mother lived? Yes, I did. The truth was that I had too many lines and electrodes hooked to both arms to manage a keyboard. Unaware that *I* was the patient in this picture, my editor agreed to overnight a hard copy to Milwaukee.

She hoped we could turn it around in a week.

"Sure, why not?" I replied. The blood pressure monitor beeped.

MY BRAIN EVENT III

The Final Episode

MAY 2012

As a writer, I have had the good fortune of working with a brilliant editor at W. W. Norton and Company, the publisher of my first two novels. When Alane takes on a project, you can be sure that she believes very strongly in it, that she has many intelligent ideas about how to make the book the best it can be, and that she's willing to spend as much time and effort as it takes to accomplish exactly that. Another one of her authors has compared Alane's editorial guidance to the "tenacious cajoling" of a boxing coach.

I can identify, especially with the boxing coach part.

As a patient in the Neurosurgical ICU in a hospital in Milwaukee in October 2009, I was also lucky, having suffered no apparent damage from my "small stable bleed." In fact, I would have been sent home to Iowa after three days, if it hadn't been for the peculiar shape of certain arteries in my brain. Those who know me are probably not surprised to learn of peculiarities in my brain. These oddities—though not necessarily hazardous—made my first angiogram inconclusive. Sentenced to another week of observation, I graduated from the ICU to the "Neuro" floor to await a second angiogram.

So there I was, still under fairly strict rest-and-relaxation orders on the Neuro floor, when a package arrived from New York.

"Don't open it!" my husband said.

We knew what was inside: my novel manuscript, its pages festooned with yellow post-its stuck there by my editor, every one of which would ask me to cut, change, or clarify something. It's business as usual for an author, this responding to your editor's queries (as the complaints and questions on the post-its or in the margins are politely called). You just grit your teeth and go through them, query by query, making changes that seem well advised and rejecting suggestions that don't. These you mark "STET," making your case on the post-it in your own cramped handwriting (or on a separate sheet if you need more space) as to why the editor should "let it stand."

Business as usual, yes, but not always good for the blood pressure. A mere phone call from my editor earlier that week had sent the numbers soaring on the monitor over my head. (How glad I was to have escaped the Neurosurgical ICU, where your every thought and feeling registered on a screen somewhere. You might as well be wearing your heart on your sleeve — if hospital gowns can be said to have sleeves.) I reminded John that Alane said she needed the manuscript back in a week or less.

"Don't open it!" he said. Good advice, I had to admit, but in that case, what to do?

Enter our daughter Liz, Editor Extraordinaire.

Liz had read every page of every draft of my novel, even in its most unwieldy forms. She had saved the life of one of the characters by threatening never to read another word if I killed him off. Liz knew what I had written — and what I wished I had written — at least as well as I did. She made the eight-hour drive from Omaha that weekend, rushing to my bedside with her own supply of color-coded post-its, soon to be stuck alongside every editorial query: pink for STET, orange for changes accepted on my behalf, and the smallest smattering of peaceful blue ones calmly recommending that I take a look at *these* queries, just these few, that's all.

It was a little strange, my husband said later, to be holed up with Liz in a visitor's lounge while I had my second angiogram, the two of them working their way, slowly and carefully, through the pages of my novel, even as the neurosurgeon was making his way, slowly and carefully, through my brain. But heck. What is a work of fiction, after all, if not a manifestation on paper of the peculiar workings of the author's brain?

When you've spent ten days in the neurosurgical department of a hospital hundreds of miles from your home (half of it in the ICU) all you care to notice about your second angiogram, the one that gives you the all clear, is the good news: "no new areas," "no new findings," "no evidence for aneurysm," and the ever-insulting "brain is otherwise unremarkable." There was no need for stents in my arteries or holes drilled in my head—nothing but a follow-up appointment in Iowa City and a third and final angiogram three or four months down the road.

A few more adventures lay ahead. We'd been back in Iowa City for a day or two—the manuscript mailed off in plenty of time—when I noticed that little red target-like spots had begun to appear on all parts of me. We made two trips on two successive days to the ER, where everyone seemed surprised that Benadryl and more Benadryl wasn't helping. I was allergic to something, probably the angiogram dyes. By the third day, what at first looked like extra-puffy hives on my face had blended together into a perfectly round, pink, baby face that was not recognizable as me. (Now, too late, I wish I'd let my husband take a picture.)

On the third trip to the ER they decided that what I had was erythema multiforme, or a "various red rash." When I asked what kind of treatment was required—the Benadryl wasn't working, I reminded the ER doc—he looked grim.

"There's nothing we can do," he said.

This was the worst moment of my whole brain event. In the long pause that followed, I imagined how different my life would be now that I looked like an alien from the Babyface Planet.

And then the other doctor said, "It will just go away by itself."

When I had a follow-up angiogram in February 2010, the rash and puffiness returned, though mildly. I was advised by the presiding neurosurgeon to steer clear of neurosurgeons for the foreseeable future, advice that I have followed faithfully. In March, I mailed the final page proofs of *The Cailiffs of Baghdad, Georgia* back to the publisher. The book came out in September, a little less than a year after my brain event. I'm told I looked perfectly normal as I signed books at the bookstore.

Maybe you were there?

WRITING PROMPTS

Write Your Own Six-Minute Memoirs

Here are a few ideas to get you started on your own six-minute memoirs. You'll think of many more. I have included some essay titles in case you want to see where such a prompt led me.

Write about a time when

a stranger came to your rescue ("Infrequent Flyer"; "I Love New York")

you were involved in a verbal misunderstanding, international or otherwise ("I See London, I See France")

your father or mother (or the authority figure of your choice) did something ill advised ("Hornet Wars")

you were scared to death and nobody knew it ("What Did I Say?"; "Where the Girls (and Boys) Are")

you had to sit very still ("Infrequent Flyer")

your children (or you) were at that in-between age — old enough to go off the diving board and young enough to want somebody there to see it when they did ("Night Swimming"; "On Baby Watch"; "Mother and Child Reunion")

you found — or put — something unusual in your pocket ("Now There Is a Miracle")

something happened that seemed like a miracle — or was one! ("Now There Is a Miracle")

you solved a problem in an especially resourceful or creative way ("Aquila Non Capit Muscas")

you accomplished something you didn't know you could do
   ("Where the Girls (and Boys) Are"; "Hysterical Preservation,
   Parts I–III")

you tried something new ("Scuba: Do? (or Don't)")

it was hard to let go ("The End of the World as We Know It";
   "Sitting in the Lonely Seat on the Long Way Home")

Bring to life on the page

a person who has inspired you — to do better, to be happier, etc.
   ("Saturdays with Sarah"; "Remembering Ellen"; "From the
   Locker Room")

a person — or a place — that surprised you ("From the Locker
   Room"; "Mother and Child Reunion")

a pet that brought you love and trouble — or just trouble
   ("Squeaky Bites the Dust"; "Philosopher Cat for Sale")

Recreate a moment from

a trip you took with your mother or an equally challenging
   traveling companion ("Mother and Child Reunion")

a visit to (or from) a relative that you don't see very often or
   perhaps never previously met at all ("Great Aunts"; "Photo
   Opportunities")

the years — or days or merely hours — you spent learning a
   particular skill ("Paradise Lost")

a shopping experience you are not likely to forget ("The Right
   Clothes"; "Infrequent Flier")

Describe

a photo you wish you had taken — or one that you have lost
   ("Photo Opportunities")

a procedure or process you have performed—possibly on yourself—or one you have undergone ("Are We Really Worth It?"; "Cardiac Dreams"; "Hysterical Preservation, Parts I–IV"; "My Brain Event, Parts I–III")

the first neighborhood (or house or kitchen) you can remember ("Positively 4th Street"; "Hornet Wars"; "King of Scrounge")

your favorite backyard ("In My Own Backyard")

a place you visited only once (or twice) but have never forgotten ("What's in a Name"; "If It's Tuesday, This Must Be Hong Kong")

ACKNOWLEDGMENTS

The note to readers at the beginning of this book thanks some of the key players in the story that led to the book in your hands: Claudia Mueller, Dennis Reese, the *Iowa Source* and Iowa Public Radio, the Johnson County Senior Center (now The Center) for inviting me to teach a writing course that gave me the blueprint for my own essays, and the "seniors" who wrote along with me in the course.

To that short list I'd like to add the University of Iowa Press—in particular, the enthusiastic and patient editorial team who worked with me to turn these selections from more than twenty years of monthly columns into a book. My thanks go to James McCoy, Meredith Stabel, Susan Hill Newton, Allison Means, Karen Copp, Tegan Daly, and Rebecca Marsh. Special thanks to Holly Carver, Bur Oak series editor, for leading the way.

The book is dedicated to everyone who appears in it, and to every one of them, I am grateful. I wish I could list all of them here by name.

For multiple appearances in the essays and for their unfailing support off the page, I thank my husband John; my son Jeff and daughters Liz and Lauren; and my grandchildren—precocious and adorable at every age—David and Vanessa. Monika and Van: thank you, too!

For more than twenty years' worth of faith in my work and for her diligent efforts to get it out there into the world, I once again thank my agent, Valerie Borchardt.

And although I have thanked Claudia Mueller—editor and publisher of the *Iowa Source* throughout its thirty-seven-plus years (so far) of publication—for providing me with an audience and the occasion to write these pieces, I want to add my gratitude for the unexpected gift that writing the column gave me. I might never have known how much fun I have in my life, if it weren't for this opportunity to write it all down.

BIBLIOGRAPHY

Alighieri, Dante. *Inferno.* Translated by Robert Hollander and Jean Hollander. New York: Anchor Books, 2002.

Barthelme, Donald. "The Dolt." In *Sixty Stories*, 83–89. New York: Penguin Books, 2003.

Borges, Jorge Luis. "Borges and I." Translated by James E. Irby. In *Labyrinths*, 246–47. New York: New Directions, 2007.

Calvino, Italo. *Invisible Cities.* Translated by William Weaver. San Diego: Harcourt, 1978.

Cervantes Saavedra, Miguel de. *Don Quixote.* Translated by John Ormsby. Chap. 8 in *The Bedford Anthology of World Literature, Book 3: The Early Modern World, 1450–1650.* Boston: Bedford/St. Martin's, 2004.

The Chinese Book of Songs. Translated by Arthur Waley. New York: Grove Press, 1960.

Columbus, Christopher. *The Log of Christopher Columbus.* Translated by Robert H. Fuson. Blue Ridge Summit, PA: International Marine/ TAB Books, 1992.

DeFrees, Madeline. *Blue Dusk: New and Selected Poems, 1951–2001.* Port Townsend, WA: Copper Canyon Press, 2001.

Derrida, Jacques. *Of Grammatology.* Translated by Gayatri C. Spivak. Baltimore: Johns Hopkins University Press, 1976.

Dickinson, Emily. *The Complete Poems of Emily Dickinson.* Edited by Thomas H. Johnson. Boston: Little, Brown, 1960.

Giamatti, A. Bartlett. *A Great and Glorious Game.* Chapel Hill: Algonquin Books, 1998.

Hampl, Patricia. *I Could Tell You Stories: Sojourns in the Land of Memory.* New York: W. W. Norton, 1999.

Keyes, Margaret N. *Nineteenth Century Home Architecture of Iowa City.* Iowa City: University of Iowa Press, 1966.

Milosz, Czeslaw. *New and Collected Poems: 1931–2001.* New York: HarperCollins, 2001.

Munro, Alice. "Leaving Maverly." In *Dear Life*, 67–90. New York: Alfred A. Knopf, 2012.

O'Connor, Flannery. "On Her Own Work." In *Mystery and Manners: Occasional Prose*, 107–118. New York: Farrar, Straus, and Giroux, 1969.

Salinger, J. D., "For Esmé—with Love and Squalor." In *Nine Stories*, 87–114. Boston: Little, Brown, 1981.

Saussure, Ferdinand de. *Course in General Linguistics*. Edited by Perry Meisel and Haun Saussy. Translated by Wade Baskin. New York: Columbia University Press, 2011.

Simonite, Tom. "The Quest to Put More Reality in Virtual Reality." *Technology Review*, October 22, 2014. https://www.technologyreview .com/2014/10/22/170645/the-quest-to-put-more-reality-in-virtual -reality/

Tennyson, Alfred, Lord. "In Memoriam A. H. H." Canto 56. London: Edward Moxon, 1850.

Welty, Eudora. "A Worn Path." In *The Collected Stories of Eudora Welty*, 142–51. New York: Harcourt, 1982.